Tales from the Toe Tag Chaplain

By
Joseph P. Smith

Tales from the Toe Tag Chaplain
© 2013 by Joseph P. Smith

IFCA Press is an imprint of
IFCA International
PO Box 810
Grandville, MI 49468-0810

All rights reserved

Requests for permission to quote from this book should be directed to IFCA International, Department of Hospital Chaplains - 616-531-1840 Ext 307 or Fax 616-531-1814

Cover Design and Photography by
Kara Hanes Photography
3839 White ST. SW Grandville MI 49418
616-835-6143
www.KaraHanesPhotography.com

Except for some quotations from the King James Version in dialog, all Scripture quotations are from the New American Standard Bible, Copyright © 1960, 1962, 1963, 1968, 1971, 1972, 1973, 1975, 1977, 1995, by The Lockman Foundation.

ISBN-13: 978-1493550166

For Nancy
fifty-one years a faithful partner

Dedicated to
John VanderSchie
My Chaplaincy Mentor

Special thanks to Marsha Hornok who did the hard work of a book editor quickly. Marsha is an accomplished magazine editor

Thanks to my very professional granddaughter Kara Haynes, for her cover design and photography.

I also thank Trinka Jeffery for helping me with Microsoft Word.

Contents

Chapter 1 Faith Sized Prayers	1
Chapter 2 A Chaplain's Job Description	7
Chapter 3 Useful Silliness	16
Chapter 4 Right and Left Brained People	35
Chapter 5 Denial or Victory	42
Chapter 6 A Deist Gets Personal	49
Chapter 7 Learning the Ropes	57
Chapter 8 No Blank Tablets	60
Chapter 9 A Heart of Condemnation	66
Chapter 10 The Challenge of Abortion	73
Chapter 11 Setting Captives Free (or not)	79
Chapter 12 A Job Description Adjustment	87
Chapter 13 Victory Over Self	97
Chapter 14 Baseball Babies	105
Chapter 15 An Identity Crisis	111
Chapter 16 Attempted Exorcism	120
Chapter 17 Unpardonable Sin	125
Chapter 18 The Child Bride	131
Chapter 19 The Bible Battle	137
Chapter 20 Preventing Divorce	140
Chapter 21 The Bat Boy	146
Chapter 22 Come Out!	150
Chapter 23 The Runaway Son	158
Chapter 24 American Gothic	164
Chapter 25 A Genteel Lady	170
Chapter 26 A Houseful of Antiques	177
Chapter 27 The Sobbing Doctor	186
Chapter 28 Caroling, Caroling	192

Introduction

I held the hands of more than a hundred people while they died, and it became the joke of the hospital that it wasn't smart to hold my hand. That's how I earned the name, "Toe Tag Chaplain." For eight years, I served the sixty bed Oncology Unit in a downtown hospital in Grand Rapids, Michigan.

I have been in Christian ministry for more than fifty years, and if I had to tell 100 interesting anecdotes from those 50 years, 90 of them would come from that chaplaincy. It was better than an education; in fact, it was my education in listening to the core of the human condition. Every day I learned an adventurous lesson, often filled with tragedy. I gained a constant source of inspiration as I watched medical personnel bravely serving in the worst arena of physical sickness, exercising their healing arts.

The professionals taught me much, but patients taught me even more. They struggled to survive dashed dreams and uncertain outcomes. I watched them somehow cope, often using mechanisms that not to my liking and counter to good spiritual reality. This gave me insights few ministry professionals encounter. Oncology patients rarely play games. Reality, grim reality, has a way of cutting through the charades in which most people live.

I don't want you to think the treatments were futile; most patients survived, and many more had life extended until they died of something other than cancer. But as Susan Sontag pointed out in her book *Illness as Metaphor*, cancer is a dreary word. Consumption (Tuberculosis) compares to physical wasting and spiritual victory as in Dickens' writings, but cancer as a metaphor compares to urban blight. It's hard to think of victories in a department where as many as three out of sixty patients were designated as DNR (do not resuscitate). It took some adjusting to look for bright spots in these shades of gray.

In the midst of all this, heaven poured out blessings. Often, answers from God that ultimately bless are not what we anticipate. But His way is perfect, and its inevitable outcome a heaven that is just and where the inhabitants are like Christ.

"...And all things you ask in prayer, believing, you will receive."
Matthew 21:22

Chapter 1
Faith Sized Prayers

On entering the room, I encountered the spectacle of a technician making a small incision in Charlie's arm to start a morphine drip into a deep vein. I excused myself, saying I could come back later, but Charlie asked me to stay and the technician told me to stay away from the wound. While he continued his work, I asked Charlie to tell me what he knew about God, and how he had learned it.

At the age of eight, Charlie had been sent by his parents to live with and work for a neighbor during harvest season. After harvest ended he walked home only to find his parents gone. Abandoned by his parents, he managed to survive childhood without adult help. But he was always plagued by the idea that there must be something terribly wrong with him, because even his parents didn't love him. So he became a recluse. However, he managed to get married and that union produced a lovely little girl who was the joy of his lonely life.

Missionaries from Michigan's Rural Bible Mission held regular Bible classes in the girl's school. They were known as "Uncle" or "Aunt" so one day she stayed after class so Uncle Mel could tell her how Jesus had made sure she could go to heaven. But after professing faith, she seemed so sad that Uncle Mel asked her why.

"I love my daddy," she said, "but he doesn't know what you just told me!"

Uncle Mel got her address and that night called on Charlie. He must have been a good communicator, because a generation later, Charlie was crystal clear about the Gospel, and even though he had never been to church, sure of his heavenly destination.

I wondered if he could read, but I offered him a copy of *Our Daily Bread*, a booklet of daily devotionals. I wanted to do more for Charlie, and I offered to pray for him.

"No one's done that for me since Uncle Mel." he said. "But sure, I don't see why not."

It's my conviction that in audible prayer, it's important to engage the other in the prayer, but I was very doubtful that Charlie could feel comfortable actually talking to God out loud, so I adjusted to a backup plan and asked him what he wanted me to pray for.

"I've never thought about that," Charlie said.

"Ok, let's start by asking what you need now, and then, what can you believe God can do for you," I rejoined.

"Praying for what I need is new to me," Charlie said, "When my parents were gone, I figured it was all up to me. If I wanted a helping hand, I found it at the end of my right arm."

That's a clever turn of phrase. I marveled at the eloquence of this guy who had no "upbringing." Obviously, prayer wasn't a familiar practice. And that seemed incongruous. How could he be so sure that God would take him to heaven, but and never engage God in conversation?

"We could start with praying about your treatment," I suggested, "and then for whatever else you need. The fact that you're starting a morphine drip tells me that you're in serious medical trouble."

Charlie turned away as he spoke. "I know the cancer's going to get me. It doesn't seem right to pray to be healed."

"God can do that, Charlie, but He might not. The question is, 'What can you believe God will do for you.' We can pray 'faith sized' requests. Let's not pray for a million bucks, or the moon with a fence around it."

"I know this cancer is going to get me," he repeated, "but I want to die in my right mind. I don't want to be crazy with pain, or lose control of myself. And then, I'd like to see Uncle Mel again."

I couldn't help noting how important control was to him, and I understood why. But to see "Uncle" Mel, again! That was a tall order. Since Charlie said he could trust God for it, I faithfully, but with limited faith, prayed for that. On a Tuesday morning!

It was Thursday before I got back to him. As I came in the door, his first words were, "You found him!"

I had forgotten his prayer request, so I said, "Found who?"

"Uncle Mel!" he responded, "and he lives 150 miles into Canada."

The border was 180 miles from us! "He came here to see me yesterday!"

"I didn't find him," I replied. "God must have sent him." I couldn't imagine how it had happened. If this wasn't a miracle, it was certainly an unusual coincidence.

It was later explained by a telephone operator at the hospital. She manned an information station near the main door, and knew Uncle Mel from years ago.

"Yesterday he came looking for a sick relative in our hospital, and decided to check the clergy box. He saw Charlie's name and remembered him from one solitary meeting." God's miracles don't use the supernatural as much as the remarkable.

The medical people did wonders for Charlie. They were able to regulate that morphine drip so that he was relatively pain-free without being sedated, until he died about two weeks later, with God graciously answering his prayer requests. Charlie died in an afternoon after a morning playing checkers with his grandson.

Charlie's world was a small one, where his primary instinct never got beyond survival. He had likely never traveled outside the five-county area where he was born and died. His life experiences were difficult and certainly not opulent. He had a well-loved wife, a beautiful daughter, a bright grandson and a generous God. Somehow our wonderful God opened the door that his xenophobia had nailed shut, and let me in for a little time, for which I am grateful.

Pure and undefiled religion in the sight of
our God and Father is this:
to visit orphans and widows in their distress,
and to keep oneself unstained by the world.
James 1:27

Chapter 2
A Chaplain's Job Description

The name beside the door gave me a clue to the patient's age. It's been a while since mothers named daughters Bertha. She had transferred in from a smaller hospital to see if the Grand Rapids Clinical Oncology program could do more for her. My call slip indicated she had liver cancer.

A chaplain has to be careful to identify his reason for calling on someone who's been sick for some time, or his very presence may be interpreted as a medical prognosis. The call slip didn't give me any information I wouldn't have from observing her, because I could see the outline of that distended organ elevating the bed covers.

Joseph P. Smith

"Hi. I'm the chaplain for this floor, and I call on all the new patients to see if they would appreciate any spiritual help. I love, for instance, to pray with my patients. Tell me, if I were to pray for you today, what would you like me to pray for?"

"I'm chicken," she said.

This dismissive expression seemed unusual for a woman of her age. That signaled that she couldn't even bring herself to talk about how serious her concerns were. I would need to spell out the real meaning of her response.

"You're afraid," I said. "Is this a general sense of fear, or is there some one thing you're afraid of."

"Death," was her monosyllabic response. Any more than that one word was impossible for her.

To probe further, I offered her some options. "Some people are afraid of losing things they have treasured. Others fear the process of dying. And some wonder what comes after death."

"All three." Again her response was as short as possible.

Tales from The Toe Tag Chaplain

"What are the things you think you will miss the most?

"My husband, my children, my home. I guess you could say my life."

I responded, "Those are all things that are good gifts from God. The fact that you will miss them shows how good God has been to you. But there are only two kinds of lives. One is a life filled with good things from God, and in the end, those people will have to miss them for a while. The other is a life with nothing good in it. Those people have nothing to lose. Evidently, you've had the better option."

"As to the process of dying, I can't tell you what that is like. I've never done it, and neither has anyone who can tell you about it, but I can tell you one thing. We won't run away from you. We'll do our best to see that you don't face it alone."

Then for what comes after death, God has prepared a way for you to know that you don't need to be frightened about it. Jesus went ahead of us to prepare a place more beautiful than you can imagine. We don't deserve it, but He wants us to have it so much that He suffered all that we deserve so that we can be sure God doesn't need any more penalty from us. What He does ask is that we trust Jesus and what He did in His passion as sufficient to take us to heaven."

"I'd like to be sure of something," she said.

"You've probably heard that Jesus died in your place on the cross. He paid for your sin so that He could say, 'God so loved the world that He gave his one and only son, so that whoever believes in Him will not perish, but have everlasting life.' If He would do that for you, there's no reason that you should not trust Him."

"I hope that's so," she said

I replied, "There's no better One to trust. He died for you, and to prove God accepted His sacrifice, He rose again from the dead."

She brightened a little and said, "I'm so glad you came today. God must have sent you just for me! This is what I needed to hear!"

She seemed happier than when I came. I wondered if this brief description of the Gospel was enough, but I strongly felt she wasn't ready for more, and I couldn't understand my feelings. So after I prayed that God would give her understanding of His saving plan, and confidence in His goodness to calm her fears, I made a mental note to follow up the next day, and went about my rounds.

The next day when I came into the room, she was in obvious distress. I greeted her, and she replied, but she avoided looking at me. There was something on her mind, something she had a hard time telling. To give her time, and confidence that I had time for her, I pulled up a hard chair by the bed and sat down. The room got quiet.

When she finally looked at me she said almost in a whimper, "Do you really think God could forgive me?"

"Yes, I really do."

"But you don't know me."

"That's true, but I do know Him!"

Tears streaming down her face she said, "I've never told anyone this. My husband doesn't know. I never even told my priest. I had six children in seven years, and was pregnant with the seventh. I told my neighbor I couldn't take anymore, and she told me how to get rid of it. I tried. I didn't succeed. But every time I look at my beautiful son, I say to myself, 'You tried to kill him.'"

Her records didn't show she was a Catholic. Most Catholics, even those with the most tenuous claim to that status, identify as Catholics at intake. But her self-condemning mind wouldn't allow that. She was sure that her antipathy about her pregnancy, and her plan to end it, had condemned her.

"God doesn't enjoy punishing anyone," I said. "The Bible says He is not willing that any should perish. A famous writer once said that every face you see walking down the street represents someone who will one day be a glorious saint in the eternal presence of God, or a miserable wretch in hell. God prefers the former. David killed Bathsheba's husband so his sin of adultery wouldn't be found out. And later God called him a man after his own heart. Saul, who became the apostle Paul, held the coats of the mob that stoned Stephen to death. He would later say, 'For me to live is Christ, and to die is gain, even though he called himself the chief of sinners'

"God is more concerned with what we become than what we have done. Of course, our sins deserve terrible punishment, but that's why Jesus, who was God the Son, became a man and suffered the punishment in our place. And God showed us that He accepted Jesus' substitutionary sacrifice by raising Him from the dead. You can be made clean by that very act. You only need to trust Jesus."

"I can't believe it's that easy," she said.

"Easy for you, but not for Him." I replied. "He loved you so much; He was willing to go to the cross so you could spend eternity with Him. That certainly wasn't easy. Sin deserves eternal punishment. But God doesn't enjoy damnation. He allowed Jesus to die in your place so you wouldn't have to pay for your sins yourself. If we don't trust what He has done for us, then His dying purpose was thwarted. He loves you! Don't you get it? He really loves you!"

She didn't respond verbally, but she reached out to take my hand, and I prayed that she would be convinced that God loved her, and that she could trust Him.

When the prayer was finished, she didn't want to let go. I rose from the chair, and we stood smiling at each other until finally her grip loosened and I left.

The next time I came back, she seemed despondent again. To allow her to tell me what was on her mind I said, "Bertha, how are things?"

She spoke as if defeated, "I'm going home."

"But you don't seem happy about it."

"No. The tumor has grown and I can't get my dress on. I'll have to go home in a hospital gown."

It was time for a job description adjustment for me. Was her wardrobe my responsibility? No, but her dignity was. "Where is the dress?" I asked.

"In the locker, there."

It was a fairly straight dress, made to pull over but with a fitted waist. And there was a seam in the back. A cardigan sweater was on the hook by it.

I said, "You know, I'll bet we can open up this seam at the waist, and after you get it on, we can cover that with the sweater. I'll see if a nurse has a tool that can do it."

I found a handy LPN with scissors, told her what to do, and let them have some privacy. Later, I saw her in a wheelchair, well dressed and carrying some flowers she had received, being wheeled to the car that would take her home. She waved, and smiled. I never saw her again. But I believe I will see her in heaven!

The full range of a Chaplain's ministry can never be delimited in a job manual. It is a rich opportunity to serve in all kinds of ways.

A joyful heart is good medicine,
But a broken spirit dries up the bones.
Proverbs 17:22

Chapter 3
Useful Silliness

The handsome, sunny guy was only seventeen. My first sight of Brian* was with his gown pulled aside, and his pajama bottoms pushed down to the edge of decency. His mother hovered over him holding a tincture of Methylate bottle. He was dipping a q-tip in the bottle and carefully painting on his stomach.

"What are you doing!?" I asked.

"I'm having a splenectomy this afternoon," he replied.

"So?"

"I'm leaving a message for the OR," he said.

The pink tincture spelled out the words; *please do not open until Christmas.*

Here was a new face of denial.

Tales from The Toe Tag Chaplain

It's not my job to shake people like Brian into being serious. I have come to believe that denial is a gift from God. It enables people to function for a while so they can cope when reality is suddenly too grim to bear. It's like a fuse in an electrical circuit. It opens the circuit when the electrical load is too much for the system. You shouldn't "fix" it. In fact, if the load is too much to bear, closing the circuit of reality can do great damage.

But humor was an unusual face of denial. However for the medical team, it was a delight in our often dreary experience. Brian quickly became the talk of the unit. Nothing about his case could be too serious if he was having so much fun.

Then, when chemotherapy began, he waited until lights out, pulled the covers up to his chin, put on a full head rubber ape mask, and went to sleep. This was in the days before positive pressure pumps were common for infusions, so the I.V. bag had a piece of tape on its side, marked with the time when the drip rate should allow the fluid to reach that level. The night nurse came in with her flashlight up on the bag to check the flow, then down the tube to see if there was any blood infiltration, and then up to the face to check the patient's skin color. Imagine her surprise to find an ape in the bed!

After that, there were the rubber snakes under the covers. Then rubber tarantulas on the bed frame. He just never seemed to take his condition seriously, and all of us enjoyed his pranks.

He got into remission, and then pulled the ultimate stunt. He got a nurse to bring an empty I.V. bag, clamped the tube shut so it wouldn't leak, and taped the tube to the back of his hand to look like there was a needle there. Then he cut a little slit near the hanger to fill the bag with tap water, hung it on a portable I.V. pole, put a goldfish in the bag, and pushed it all over the hospital! That's major creativity!

One of the oncology residents decided to get back at him, so she told him he couldn't go home without an allergy test.

"What's that!" he asked.

"Well, we tape a paper template on your back where the skin isn't very sensitive, and poke different allergens under your skin following the pattern on the paper.

TALES FROM THE TOE TAG CHAPLAIN

You'll just feel like you're being poked, because of the insensitivity there. Then, if you react to any of them, we can tell by the pattern what you're allergic to."

She got him to lay face down on the treatment table, taped some paper on his back, and commenced to poke around. Finished, she ripped the paper off and threw it in the wastebasket. He rose and asked, "Can I look at it in the mirror?"

"By all means," she replied.

He got his back to the mirror, turned to look, and saw "Gotcha!" in psychedelic paint with the letters reversed on his back!

He didn't take it well. He thought he was supposed to hand out the stunts, not receive them. So he got his mother to scrub the paint off, which left an outline of the word, and then got her to put Methylate dots on the outline. Calling a nurse in, he asked her to tell the resident that he had broken out from her paint.

"I can't tell her that," the nurse said. "It's a lie."

"Well, tell her I have red specs where the paint was, and I'm itching like mad." And he began scratching to substantiate the deception.

The poor resident thought her career was done. But nothing ever came of it, and he went home, still everybody's hero.

It was six months before I saw again. The remission had lasted long enough for his hair to come back, and it was now as curly as if it was permed. But things quickly got serious. He began to spike high fevers, and to keep from brain damage, suffered cooling alcohol baths, and finally an ice water mattress. Pain came with such irregularity it wasn't well controlled. His platelet count went down and he began to bleed in crazy places.

There was a teen-aged friend who cut school to be at Brian's side. He wasn't as bright as our patient, but he could have won a prize for his loyalty. Then one day when the friend wasn't there, I decided to sit quietly beside the bed until the cut-up spoke.

His first words after a long wait were, "It doesn't look good, does it?"

"No, it doesn't." I said, "We never give up hope, but you really can't joke your way out of this." I hoped it would be taken kindly, and it was.

"I don't want to face it." he said.

"It's not easy to face, I replied. "But what can make it easier is to know what God has promised, even if the worst happens."

A short period of quiet seemed to give me permission to go on.

"I know you go to church, so perhaps you've heard that God wants us to be confident of our eternal destiny. In John's first epistle, God says that certain things were written so we could know we have eternal life. Jesus gave Himself to us, and anyone who has Him, has the life, because real life is in Him."

"I'm not sure Jesus lives in me," he said.

"He has promised to come into anyone who invites Him," I said. "Everlasting life does not begin when you die, but when Christ comes in. He said, 'He that hears my word, and believes who sent me, has (present tense) everlasting life, and shall not (future tense) come into judgment, but is passed (already) from death to life."

He responded, "I'm not sure Jesus is in my life. I think if He were, I would feel more holy."

"It's not about how you feel. It's about what you believe. We've been quoting some of His promises to you. Do you really think He will keep them? Can you imagine that Jesus would wait all these centuries to make you the first person He ever lied to? Just for your own assurance, why don't you silently pray and ask Him into your life?"

He closed his eyes for about twenty seconds.

I said, "It seemed like you just prayed a short prayer."

"Yes."

"Did you invite Jesus into your life?"

"Yes. But I don't feel any different."

"Did He promise to come in if you asked Him to?"

"Yes."

"Does He keep his promises?"

"Yes."

"Are you sure He does?"

"Yes."

"Then it doesn't matter what you feel. Feelings can depend on what you had for dinner. But the fact is, God made a promise. And God can't lie! Believing that fact is what faith is. We just depend on His word."

" I see...." he said. I can be sure because I'm sure He doesn't lie."

"That's it. He doesn't lie," I said.

His eyes closed again, but this time it was due to exhaustion.

"I'll see you tomorrow." I said as I rose.

Brian didn't acknowledge that. He seemed to be resting peacefully. I retreated out the door without speaking again.

I had met his pastor during a hospital visit, and I urged him to take special care of Brian's parents.

Joseph P. Smith

He said, "I'm not worried about that. His parents never miss a Sunday in church."

But I worried! In the year a child dies, parental divorce is about five times the national average.

Parents often don't grieve the same way. Brian's mother was falling apart. And the father thought someone needed to hold it together. His stoic demeanor made her think he didn't care. His wife's weeping seemed un-parental to him.

The inordinate bleeding increased. One day Brian signaled for his friend to hold the bowl while he vomited. He threw up a pint of blood and died. The parents had filed for divorce. And the pastor thought it was his duty to refuse to have the funeral. It became one of the few funerals I had for a patient.

There were other unusual things about this funeral. Six of his nurses attended. He had won their hearts with his antics, making our dreary unit almost bearable.

The title of my sermon was, *Are There Any Rubber Snakes in Heaven?* And the substance of it was, maybe last week there weren't! Then I simply recounted Brian's steps to faith.

You would think the story ended there, but six months later, the telephone operator handed me a note from the medical intermediate unit saying that a patient there wanted to see me by name. I didn't know who Sam* was, but always honored such requests. But when I got to the room, the door was shut tight.

Not sure what was going on, I turned to go to the desk to ask. But there were three nurses standing in the hall, staring at the door.

"Can I go in there?" I asked.

"I wouldn't if I were you," one answered.

"Why not?"

"Well, to begin with, there's glass all over the floor!" she said.

"What happened?"

Joseph P. Smith

"He's angry, and he's throwing everything he can reach at anybody in sight."

I insisted, "He's asked to see me, and I have to try!"

"Do you have good soles on your shoes?"

I didn't answer but slowly pushed the door open. Sam was the buddy who had been holding the bowl for Brian when he died.

"They're trying to kill me," were Sam's first words.

"We don't do that here," I said, "What makes you say that?"

"They're making me sit up in this chair, and it hurts. About five more minutes of this and I'm going to die!" He said.

"I doubt that. I'd guess that some sitting is part of your treatment plan. But if you've been up a while, it might be enough. I'll go check."

"The nurses were still in the hall, maybe to watch me get thrown out. I said, "Has he been sitting up long enough?"

"Yes."

"Well let's get him back in bed."

"We can't."

Why not?"

"He's had a stroke, and his left foot will drag in the glass." I could hardly imagine a 19 year old with a cerebral hemorrhage that had his whole left side in a slack paralysis.

"Well, let's clean it up!"

"That's the sanitor's job." Boy, they really didn't want to go in there.

I said, "Get me a dust mop. And I'll hold his leg up. Don't worry, there's nothing left to throw."

I left the door open while I mopped the floor. We got him back in bed. His breathing sounded like half a sob, and his whole demeanor was wild with unchecked emotion.

Joseph P. Smith

As the nurses left, I turned to him and said, "I know you want to tell me something, but you're in no shape to talk right now. What you need is to sleep. I promise, if you get rested, I'll be back, and we can talk.

The nurses were still in the hall. "Do you know him?" one asked.

"Not really," I said, "Sam was a buddy of a patient I helped who died here. He was a frequent visitor, but I can't say I know him."

"Could you come to our nursing conference at 10 o'clock?"

"I never did that before," I said, "Why do you want that?"

"His behavior pattern before the stroke is a baseline from which we interpret his symptoms. If we don't know what he was like before, we can't understand how the stroke has changed his behavior and what that means."

"Ok. I'll come and tell you what little I know."

TALES FROM THE TOE TAG CHAPLAIN

At the appointed time I went and gave my short recitation of what I knew, and quickly excused myself. When I looked in the room Sam's mother was sitting there, quietly crying. He was asleep, curled up in the fetal position, noisily sucking his right thumb.

I motioned for his mother to follow me and we went to the visitor's lounge.

"What happened?" I asked.

"It's all my fault. After he came home from the funeral he was so sad. I kept telling him he needed to cheer up. One of his friends told him the way to do that was to take "speed." And look what happened!"

The meth had raised his blood pressure to the point where he blew a large artery in his brain.

"Oh, Mom!" I said, "You didn't do anything a concerned mother wouldn't do." (It never fails to surprise me how many times when we, who are primarily trained to teach forgiveness for sin, rather have to try to convince people that they are *not* guilty of something.)

I hugged her, patted her back, and returned with her to the room. The young man was still asleep, so assuring her I would return, I went back to my rounds.

At about 4:30 I wrapped things up on my floor and left. When I got to the room, Sam was sitting up in the bed, with erratic "sobby" breathing, but seeming in control of the paranoia.

"So, you wanted to see me?" I asked.

"Well, I really wanted to see Brian." he said, naming his friend.

"That's really important to you," I responded in my clinical pastoral habit.

"Yeah. If I only had five minutes with him!"

"I get it that's important to you, but I don't know why?" I asked.

"I did something to him, and he never knew who did it," he said.

This was no time to discuss how much people in heaven know. So I replied, "You want to confess something to him?"

"Yes sir."

"Well, you'll have to go to heaven to do that, because that's where he is."

"That's what you talked about at the funeral," he said. "I couldn't get that sermon out of my mind for a month."

I responded, "Did you ever do anything about it?"

"No," he said.

"Don't you think it's about time?"

His response was to fold his hands, close his eyes, and begin to pray aloud. I don't remember his exact words, but they were something like, "O God, I'm so sorry for all I've done, I want to go to heaven, because I want to see Brian again. Please forgive me."

I quoted Scripture to him, reminding him that God forgives all those who repent and ask for forgiveness. I did my best to give him assurance that he was forgiven. I prayed with him, and left the hospital for home.

Joseph P. Smith

I expect God will forgive me for my doubts, but when a person is so inappropriately emotional, I have a hard time taking what he says at face value. So even though it was Saturday, when I wasn't on duty, I dropped my wife at the supermarket and went back to the hospital. When I got to the Med/IM floor, his door was wide open, the bed was stripped, and two sanitors were disinfecting the hardware. Dismayed at what I thought had happened, I headed to the desk to make sure. There was a nurse there I didn't know, who looked up and asked how she could help. She probably knew I was a chaplain by my badge.

"What happened to Sam?" I asked.

"Oh he's so much better we moved him to a regular med/surg floor."

"What do you mean by better?" I asked.

"Well, yesterday he wouldn't cooperate with his treatment at all. The reason he was on this floor, wasn't because of the portable monitors, but because we needed extra help to handle him. I thought we might have to put him in restraints or something to keep him from hurting somebody. But the evening shift reported that he was cooperating with his treatment. He's still inappropriately emotional, but he's really trying to behave."

I responded, "I'm not surprised. Yesterday at 4:30 he got rid of a big spiritual debt load, and prayed to be forgiven."

"He did!" she said. "Wait – I still have his charts!"

She pulled the package in front of her, and as I peered over the counter, opened them and began to write.

"4:30 pm. *(date)* Born again!" I hadn't known this nurse was a Baptist.

I looked at the top of the page, and said, "That doctor hates God, and he's going to tell you that's not a medical note!"

She looked up grinning. "He told us to write down anything that might explain a change in behavior, and he hasn't got anything as good as this!

- - - - - - - - - - - - - - - - - - - -

One of the down-sides of hospital chaplaincy is that you can't follow up after people go home. But I accidently found out more of the story when a classmate of mine became this guy's pastor. With good treatment at a great rehab hospital, he regained about 80% of the use and strength on his left side, is now happily married, and works as a highly trained auto mechanic. It's a long story, but a most blessed ending.

*In the Gospel of John, Chapter 11,
there are two sisters,
one left brained,
one right brained
and one brother, brain dead.*

Chapter 4
Right & Left Brain People

Bill was laconic. He never used a syllable that wasn't absolutely necessary. I had often wanted to get him to tell what he was feeling, but no matter how much active listening I did, he never got near that subject. I didn't know much about his treatment, or his prognosis.

But I learned a great deal about how he thought. Bill analyzed well, and he kept abreast of the news. He seemed to welcome my reading of Scripture and prayers, but avoided any personal talk. If we chatted at all, it concentrated on fixing society and the value of reports in the news. I couldn't get him to talk about God unless God got in the newspaper.

Joseph P. Smith

Some people who study human nature call people like Bill left-brained. He's good at deduction. He learns by adding together little things he learns. He's not intuitive, but rational.

He had a dry sense of humor, and found amusement in public contradiction. Wanting to make a connection, I would try to find logical absurdities in the news, and tell him about them.

The biggest chuckle I ever got from him was when I told him about a Parent Teacher Committee I served on and our meeting with the School Superintendent. Our committee brought cultural events and all kind of arts to school assembly programs. The committee included high-powered people with great connections, and we put on some fantastic programs. We even got the Grand Rapids Symphony to come to the school and play while the children sat in the orchestra.

But we were so full of ideas that we began to wonder about the core curriculum. Were we getting in the way of the three Rs? We needed the Superintendent's input so we asked how many days and hours of classroom instruction the state required in a semester.

With that in mind, the next question was, were they required to make up snow days.

"No we're not required to make them up," he said.

"Why not?" was the follow-up.

"Because they're acts of God," he said.

I couldn't resist. "You're not allowed to talk about God in a public school," I said.

"We don't mean that literally," he murmured.

"I see," said another father. "Acts of God are anything you don't like, and can't blame on any one else!"

Bill enjoyed that. It was as close to talking about God as we got. Despite my philosophy of ministry, Bill remained opaque to me.

In my career as a chaplain, I had gone through three philosophies of ministry in patient visits. I started out with a burning agenda to properly relate people to God. That didn't last long. It often resulted in either silence or an agenda argument. I quickly realized that my patients already had an agenda, and I needed to pay attention to it.

This resulted in the second plan. "My agenda comes second." I wanted to talk about God in the midst of their context, but first I had to pay the price of listening to what they wanted to talk about. But it wasn't long before that began to feel phony too.

My final plan was to find an agenda for me within the patient's agenda. And I never could find such a place with Bill.

One day I came into the room, and Bill wasn't alone. His wife was sitting in the only chair and was quietly weeping.

"How are things, Bill," I asked.

"The doc just told me they're not going to try to cure the cancer any more. They're just going to try to make me comfortable."

"That's hard news to take," I said.

There was a pause, and then he looked up and said, "I've heard the Gospel many times, but right now I want you to repeat it as simply and clearly as you can."

I gave him the short course on soteriology. "Jesus died as your substitute to pay the penalty for your sins and offer you eternal life. He makes that available to anyone who believes in Him. Salvation is by grace, through faith. You can't earn it, and you'll never deserve it. But God makes this His gift to you simply because He loves you."

Bill was half sitting in the bed with the head of the bed cranked up. He stared intently looking at his hands, and I remained silent. His reply came only after obvious thought. He reached up to give me a handshake, and said, "I'll see ya in heaven."

It was a simple confession of faith. He wanted the facts. Just the facts. There were no tears, no emotion. But Bill was sure. I left him so he could comfort his wife.

- - - - - - - - - - - - - - - - - - - -

Another patient had been a Sunday School teacher for thirty-five years. We often talked about the things of God. She was full of heart-warming stories about the lives of the children she had taught. Her whole approach to God was intuitive. She never wasted time with logic. She was what some call right-brained.

Talking with her was a joy. I often went away from those visits so uplifted that I wondered who ministered to whom. With radiant face and excited voice she would tell me her stories. But one day her visage was somber. She told me that she had been given only weeks to live. I asked her how I could help her.

"Just tell me about Jesus. I need to really lean on Him right now. What kind of a person is He?"

This seemed strange at first. There was no way I could tell her anything new. But then I realized that her way of understanding Jesus was holistic. She saw Him as her answer. The facts weren't as important as the Factor. She trusted Him.

Then in an instant I could see why they call the first four books of the New Testament Gospels. They aren't soteriological syllogisms. Most of my evangelism courses were built on Paul's logical teaching. But the Gospel isn't propositions. It's a Person! You trust Jesus, because God has allowed you to know Him through His Word. That's why children understand the Gospel before they get the logic of it. We don't start by teaching children, "All have sinned." We start with, "God loves you, and you can trust Him."

She listened, beaming while I told one story after another of the one who was never selfish, always giving Himself, and entirely self-assessed. My thoughts of Him turned inward, and then I realized she was in a peaceful sleep, and I went on my way.

Jesus is the answer for both right and left brained people. But a chaplain needs to know how to present him to each of them.

> The last enemy that will be abolished is death.
> 1 Corinthians 15:26

Chapter 5
Denial or Victory

"I'm not concerned about heaven right now!"

The statement might seem strange coming from a Baptist Seminarian. But if you think about it, it's not strange at all. First of all, to him Heaven is a done deal. He had full assurance that because of what Jesus did on the cross, he was going to Heaven.

But there were things about which he wasn't so sure. He had spent the last six years trying to be a responsible husband and father. He had a lovely modest wife, and although I never saw them, two preschool children.

It's common for people who are serious about the things of God to think about heaven, even when a trip to heaven isn't imminent. It's the subject of most of the presentations of the Gospel. Because the Savior's paying the price of our sin involved His death, we have a perfect display of what God is doing to take us to Heaven. We trust Him to do that because it's evident in His sacrifice that He loves us. And Scripture is full of promises that Heaven awaits those who trust Him.

There are also promises that God will take care of our families, but as long as we can do it ourselves, we don't depend on Him for that. So the most prominent item in most Christian's agenda when facing death is, *who will take care of my family!* He's not thinking about where he's going, but what he's leaving undone.

Unthinking Christians can assume they know what is on the mind of the one who is dying. They're sure it's whether we can be confident of heaven. Even for people without that assurance, that's usually not the case. It's almost always unfinished business.

When I first became aware of this, I wondered why I hadn't understood it myself, and why so many others missed it too. But although I can't read minds, I'm sure where it comes from.

Joseph P. Smith

Visiting dying people reminds us that we too are mortal!

But for us, it's theoretical. For the patient, it's grim reality.

A classmate of mine, now an experienced pastor, once warned me to never ask people how they are.

I asked him, "Why not?"

"Because they tell you," he replied.

So many people say to me, "I have a hard time visiting the sick. I never know what to say."

But the truth is if you want to comfort a sick person you give more help by listening than by talking. Sick people are overflowing with new experiences that have them frightened and confused. They almost always need to talk about that. Your talking can get in the way.

Some of the seminarian's visitors talked so they didn't have to listen. They argued for the certainty of Heaven, when that wasn't his issue at all.

TALES FROM THE TOE TAG CHAPLAIN

    Not all pastors are like this, but too many are. A friend who was a Reformed Church of America pastor got non-Hodgkin's Lymphoma. He ministered for his last 11 years without any feeling in his hands or feet. And he told a number of us about what happened when he first reported his illness at a meeting of his Classis.

    Three of his fellow pastors came calling the next day. The first one told non-stop jokes. His humor might have been appreciated if it wasn't used to make sure my friend didn't say anything!

    The next one began reading Scripture. He went on and on. My friend, who was a good student of Scripture first got nervous, and then irritated. He began to ask himself, "I've invested my life in learning the Bible. Why am I getting angry?"

    But the fellow went on until the filibuster failed, and then quickly prayed, and left. My friend never got in a sentence.

    The third felt it was his duty to extol the death event. He raved about heaven. He finally said, "Every time I look at a coffin, I wish it were me!"

Joseph P. Smith

My friend said, "I wish it were, too!" and pushed him out of the door.

Sad feelings are never dealt with unless the sad ones are allowed to be authentic. Anyone who tries to induce feelings that are not real can never get through the ones that are! You can't have victory over fears you are never allowed to feel. The phony joy that is pasted on top of inner turmoil is not victory, but denial. My seminarian was constantly urged by fellow pastors and professors to be thrilled with his imminent home going. He was not well served.

His immune system was terribly compromised. And lurking near his nerve endings was the Herpes Zoster virus, contracted in childhood Chicken Pox. He broke out in Shingles from the top of his bald head to the soles of his feet. His pain terribly affected his wife. She couldn't bear to watch it. I couldn't either.

I remember one day slipping in the soiled linen room, closing the door, and telling God I didn't like what He was doing! What was the point in this!

And then, as a week or so went by and the shingles outbreak faded, he broke out with cold sores in all those same places. I believe God knows what He is doing and wants us to trust Him even when what he allows isn't pleasant, but those were days of great conflict for me and everybody else.

Then, over one weekend he left the hospital. I never inquired about what happened. I never saw an obituary. He was just gone.

But the thing I was left with was that all the attempts to make him appear victorious over fear and pain didn't in the least inspire the staff who had a hard time trusting God.

Then there was a little widow from a small nearby town. She was a believer, but she was scared to death. She didn't talk much, but was grateful for the care she received. She did everything that was asked of her. She didn't pray publicly. Her Gideon Bible was untouched. She often cried out with pain. She hated needles. But she thanked those who served her; she never refused what they wanted to do; and she made things as comfortable for others as possible.

Joseph P. Smith

What stood out was that she was authentic. Everyone loved her. There would often be tears in her eyes at the end of my prayers. She listened all day to Christian radio. My feeling was that she had a lot to teach those teachers. Her life was an eloquent sermon. And she never went to seminary.

No one has seen God at any time;
the only begotten God
who is in the bosom of the Father,
He has explained Him.
John 1:15

Chapter 6
A Deist Gets Personal

The stale routine was that I would come into the private room, offer to pray and read Scripture, and receive a nod from the patient who was intent on the television. The bed was always cranked up into a sitting position and the TV Guide open in his lap. He was either engrossed in the boob tube, or what program to watch next. We never made a connection. He never even turned his head.

Then one day I had a chaplain intern with me, and the T.V. was off. I was determined to end this charade of ministry.

"Craig*," I said, "I've been coming in here and reading Scripture and praying, but we never seem to make any connection. You always give permission, but it's like you're not really interested. So I want to suggest a new deal. I won't pray for you any more until you tell me what to pray for."

"Well, I never told you this, because it was easier just to let you do your thing, but I don't believe in a personal God," he replied.

I was properly rebuked. He was right. I was just doing my thing. But on the other hand, his indifference didn't help.

"Sounds like you believe in some kind of a God," I tried to explore.

He looked out of the window and since we were on an upper floor, saw the green top of a tree with a starkly red cardinal sitting in it.

"Of, yeah, that stuff out there didn't just happen," he said.

I was only trying to keep the conversation going, but I said, "How do you like the world your God made?"

"It's an awful place!" he responded.

"A minute ago, when you were looking out of the window, I saw real appreciation."

"Oh well, that stuff is OK. But I got fired from my job and my insurance was cancelled just before I was diagnosed with a brain tumor. I don't know how we're ever going to pay for all this! If people would just do what they should, the world would be wonderful. But they don't. And that makes it awful."

It was my opportunity to say, "Craig, you're now talking about right and wrong, as if there was some moral law in the universe. If there is no personal God, who made up the rules?"

The question stunned him. His first response was to get quiet, thinking, and then to weakly respond, "I never thought of that."

"Well, Craig, I understand you don't believe in a personal God, but I do. Do you mind if I pray to my personal God for you?"

"Can't hurt," was his terse reply.

My prayer focused on his concern about the cost of his treatment. I particularly avoided the cosmological issue he was wrestling with. After the prayer, I shook his hand and we left.

I nearly had an altercation in the hall with the Intern. "You really shot a hole in his thinking," he said. "You've got him going! You should have really followed up on that!"

"I'm not his enemy," I said. "I'm not here to win a debate. He's thinking! Let him think!"

Later I met his wife, and when I hinted at Craig's financial concerns, she explained that he had been a school janitor, and got caught loafing in the library. I couldn't help thinking he must have been reading Thomas Paine, the author of a popular tract used to foment the American Revolution, titled "Common Sense." Paine was a classic Deist, believing God was some eternal force that created the world, but had no personal interest in it. He wound it up, and it was running down. And I came to understand that Craig's anger over injustice was mixed with guilt.

I didn't get back to him for about four days. And when I did, his situation had changed for the worse. He was now in a double room, in the bed away from the door, and the room-darkening blinds were drawn, as was the curtain around the bed.

I'm committed to leave medical diagnoses to medical people, but you can't serve an oncology unit long without understanding what some of these things meant. He had a brain tumor, and the double images he got through his eyes were gut wrenching. Nurses darkened his environment to help him keep his dinner down. I knew he was life threatened.

So I went near the bed quietly, pulled up a chair, and just sat. It began a sort of contest, to see who would speak first. He wasn't looking at me, but he wasn't avoiding me either.

Finally he said, "You know, you're a pretty smart cookie!"

It was a nice compliment, but I had no idea in the world about how to graciously receive it. So I didn't say anything.

"Tell me something," he said, "Those twelve people who followed Jesus, were they disciples or apostles?"

Joseph P. Smith

I thought *where did that come from?* And then I saw that the Gideon Bible was open, face down on the nightstand.

"That might seem tricky, Craig, but it's really not hard. A disciple is a learner, a follower. An apostle is a sent one. They followed Jesus, and were disciples, then He sent them out, and they were apostles."

"Oh, you are a smart cookie!" he exclaimed.

I had no response.

He was looking down, maybe at his hands, maybe at the foot of the bed, but didn't speak for what seemed like an eternity. And when he did, he turned his face toward me so his wet eyes showed and said, "How does an intelligent guy come to believe in a personal God?!"

He wants to! He has too much intellectual integrity to pretend to, but he wants to!

I couldn't help thinking about my own conversion out of agnosticism. My answer was born out of that experience. "It's rather simple, Craig. It is dead certain Jesus was a person, and the record of His life confirms that He is God. I recommend that you take that Gideon Bible, and read through the entire Gospel of John. Don't get bogged down in the geography or the circumstances. Just keep asking, 'Who is this guy?' and 'Can you trust Him?'"

"I don't think I can read that much," he replied.

I believed him. "Ok, start at chapter ten and read the rest. I don't want you to miss the end of the story."

He didn't respond right away, so I took the back of his hand and prayed, then excused myself.

I don't remember why I didn't see him again for several days, but when I sat down by his bed this time, he looked right at me and said, "You'll never believe what I'm doing!"

"Oh, I don't know," I said dismissively, "I believe a lot of improbable things."

But he was serious. "Every night I pray to Jesus, and ask Him to forgive my sins!"

Joseph P. Smith

My lightheartedness did a quick turn-around. "Oh Craig, there is nothing I want more than for you to be sure He has!" And the rest of our visit was spent reviewing the promises of God to those who believe.

I left his room that day feeling less like a counselor, and more like a spectator. The verses going through my mind were:

> He said to them,
> "But who do you say that I am?"
> Simon Peter answered,
> "You are the Christ,
> the Son of the living God."
> And Jesus said to him,
> "Blessed are you, Simon Barjona,
> because flesh and blood
> did not reveal *this* to you,
> but My Father who is in heaven.
> Matthew 16:15-17

Learn to do good; Seek justice,
Reprove the ruthless, Defend the orphan,
Plead for the widow.
Isaiah 1:17

Chapter 7
Learning the Ropes

I learned this lesson through frustration. Although I had taken great pains to avoid making medical diagnoses of my patients, one area did need my medical awareness. And that was when disease caused barriers to communication. I am grateful to staff who helped me with this. It hadn't been part of my orientation training.

One patient bugged me. I would approach the bed, greet her, speak kindly, and be ignored. It was as if I wasn't there! And then one day, things came to a head. A relative across the bed from me engaged in conversation with the patient. The patient had a normal response to the visitor, but even when the relative greeted me, the patient ignored me.

Assuming she didn't want her visit with the relative to be interrupted, I simply retreated, went down the hall visiting others, but kept an eye out for when that visitor left, so I could try to minister.

After spotting the relative heading for the elevator, I interrupted my progress and went into the room again. This time there was a nurse across the bed from me. She stopped to let me speak, but again, the patient ignored me.

Frustrated, I looked up at the nurse and said, "Am I doing something wrong?"

She smiled, and without speaking came around the bed and led me by the hand to where she had been standing.

"Mrs. Austin*, this is Chaplain Smith," she said.

"How do you do, Chaplain, "said Mrs. Austin. "Why haven't you visited before now?"

Not knowing what to say, I ignored the question and offered my services. Mrs. Austin received me warmly and we had a nice visit. But the nurse stopped me later in the hall.

"Mrs. Austin has had a stroke, and one of its effects is that she's not aware of anything on her left side," she said.

I couldn't help thinking that this should have been obvious. And further reflection made me wonder how many times I talk without communicating. Real contact in communication is the responsibility of the one with the message.

I never saw Mrs. Austin again, but I frequently saw others with the same condition.

For if the bugle produces an indistinct sound,
who will prepare himself for battle?
1 Corinthians 14:8

Chapter 8
No Blank Tablets

Some barriers to communication are not physical, and a chaplain must be aware of them. We're not theoretical teachers. We aren't in front of a class, expounding systematic theology. Every communication that takes place has a context, and attempting to communicate without understanding the context can result in disaster.

This story is not about my ministry, but about something I had to deal with while directing fifteen other chaplains in six hospitals. And it happened to Beverly* who was one of our best chaplains; who was waylaid by circumstances. Yet for all that, she violated the rule that our communications are never theoretical, and that we are not writing on blank tablets.

TALES FROM THE TOE TAG CHAPLAIN

Her area of expertise was pediatrics. Her usual approach was not with theological truths, but winsome Bible stories. To this day, I have the utmost respect for her. Nevertheless, one day she innocently brought scandal to our ministry, and great hurt to a struggling mother.

Beverly was a master story teller, and also well-grounded in biblical theology. She came from a denomination known for its thorough indoctrination. And she was a product of their Christian day schools, a stellar example of them. But one unguarded moment led to disaster.

Working her way through the Pediatric Unit Beverly came to a small section designated Pediatric ICU. As she approached, she heard the head nurse inform a mother that her two-year-old daughter had acute lymphoblastic leukemia. Beverly wore a white jacket with a chaplain's shoulder patch.

The mother, in terrible distress, turned to the chaplain, buried her face in her hands, laid her head against Beverly's shoulder, crying out, "How could God do this!"

Joseph P. Smith

Bev, wounded at this understanding of God said, "God didn't do this. Sickness is in the world because of sin."

The theology behind this is that God's original creation didn't include disease. Illness entered the world as a consequence of Adam's rebellion, so it's not something God did, or does. And now, occasions of sickness are passed on to all Adam's progeny. But the mother never got that theological meaning. If it had been explained as I have, and were written on a blank tablet, it might have been eventually made clear.

But this was not a blank tablet. The mother was actually a night shift pediatric nurse. She had brought her little one to the hospital the day before, stayed with her until time to go to work, worked the night shift, gone home to get three hours of sleep and now was dead on her feet. Her distress was compounded because she was a single mother and struggling not only with the two year old, but two others. And the reason she was single was that the police had caught her husband in a sting set up to stop homosexual activity in a public rest stop. She got the news when he called to ask her to bail him out after his arrest. On the way home, she asked him how long this behavior had gone on. He told her it had started even before their marriage. She asked him if he was going to stop it. He replied that he didn't think he could.

When the news hit the papers the next morning, the parents, both his and hers, called to ask what was going on. Because he feared telling them the truth, he said the police had entrapped him and that he was not guilty. His wife was not only humiliated by the public nature of his crimes, but she felt she was a potential victim of this disease-risky behavior. Yet both her parents and his were in denial, bought the false story that it was a police set-up, and blamed her when she filed for divorce. To top it all off, they had enlisted the help of the parish priest to inform her that her soul was in peril because divorce was a sin.

So when she heard Bev say, "Sickness is in the world because of sin," she wasn't getting the theology of the origin of sin – on the contrary what she got was, "God is punishing you for the divorce by hurting your two-year-old." I can't think of a more thorough miscommunication.

Joseph P. Smith

Bev was tarred with a terrible brush. She couldn't get through her head how her innocent message had been so garbled because of the circumstances of the mother. But the fact is she didn't know enough about what was already written in that mother's consciousness to effectively communicate her message.

The question that must always guide a chaplain is, Am I sure I have listened long enough to understand what's happening? Again, our teaching is never theoretical. It's always tied to a situation. So we must sympathize, empathize, listen and explore until there's no possibility of a faux pas like this.

I ran into another such situation in which a chaplain was severely rebuked by the hospital for giving what is actually good counsel in the situation he imagined. But the reality was not what he thought.

He had entered a double room to visit one patient, but the other one, with whom he was not acquainted, asked the question. "Is it true that there is no hope of heaven for a suicide?" This question is usually asked when someone has lost a significant other to suicide. And it is important in those cases to point out that one must take into account the possibility of mental illness or diminished capacity.

But the chaplain did not notice that the questioner was keeping his hands under the bed clothes so the bandages on his wrists wouldn't show. This was not theoretical. He was asking for permission to try again. Being a hospital sponsored by a church, they weren't happy with this chaplain's first response.

He should have begun by saying, "That's a question that indicates a deep concern, and doesn't seem theoretical. I need to know what made you ask."

We will know by this that we are of the truth,
and will assure our heart before Him
in whatever our heart condemns us;
for God is greater than our heart
and knows all things. 1 John 3:19-20

Chapter 9
A Heart of Condemnation

The hospital cafeteria wasn't ideal for privacy, but the general din covered quiet conversation. So I wasn't surprised when a nurse stopped by my booth and asked, "May I sit with you?"

Ministering to staff wasn't part of a chaplain's job description, but all professionals deal with people who want "curbside" opinions. Although I don't want to interfere in a staff member's relationship with his/her pastor, there are times when help from an outsider can be useful. So I always stood ready to help staff seeking short-term intervention. "Cafeteria Counseling" wasn't unusual.

I knew this nurse's reputation as a hard-working caregiver. The downside of her personality was that she rarely smiled and carried a perpetual aura of sadness. I invited her to sit opposite me in the booth.

"I really wanted to ask you something," she said.

"Ok. I'm all ears," I answered.

"The other day I heard you say to a patient that a person could know that he was going to heaven. That doesn't seem possible to me. It's hard enough to feel forgiven for the things you've done. But also, there are things you will do, or at least might do that will need to be forgiven. Can you be sure you'll be forgiven in advance? You don't know if you'll repent and confess, asking for forgiveness."

That seemed to be quite a mouthful. So I replied, "You've thought about this a lot, haven't you? Is this a theoretical question, or are you personally concerned?"

"I guess it's personal. I try to be honest with God, but I just don't feel like I have the right to talk to Him. I try to confess my sins, but I don't feel forgiven."

"How long has this been happening?"

Joseph P. Smith

"As long as I can remember. I asked Jesus to be my Savior when I was in the Beginner's Class, but I just can't feel comfortable with God."

"Have you talked to any other pastors about this?"

"Yes. I'm a graduate of a Christian college, and I tried to figure this out with the counselor there. He didn't help. So when I graduated and went back home, I talked to my pastor. Then I talked to my husband's pastor when we were in pre-marital counseling. And when we moved here, I sought out the pastor of the church where we attend."

"That's a lot of counselors! Do I know any of them?"

She told me a long list of names, many of which I knew. All of them had a good reputation.

"Those are good pastors," I said. "If they couldn't help you, I'm not sure I can. But then, I don't know you. Tell me about yourself?"

"There's not much to tell."

"So what was growing up in your home like?" I asked.

"It was a pretty gloomy place. My father was kind to me, but he was so sad."

"You didn't mention brothers and sisters."

"No. I was an only child," she replied.

"What about your mother?" I asked.

"My mother died in childbirth."

Guess what child, I thought.

"What did these other pastors tell you?"

"They all said that Jesus had died on the cross to pay for all our sins. And we can be forgiven of all of them because the penalty for them has been paid. God is ready to forgive us if we come to Him in faith."

"Do you believe that?"

"I guess so. But why don't I feel forgiven?"

"Did anyone ever blame you for the death of your mother?"

"Oh, no. Not really. One time a neighbor told me, 'Your father must love you very much.'"

I said, "Why do you say that?"

"Because he gave the most precious thing he had for you." he said.

I sat stunned. *If all your friends were this thoughtless, you wouldn't need enemies.*

"How did your father feel about your mother's death?" I asked.

"He never got over it. He never seemed to enjoy anything. He hardly left the house except to go to work and to church. He came right home. There were many nights when he would just hold me and cry. I hugged him and patted his back, but nothing I could do made him feel any better."

I couldn't hold back the tears. I covered her hand on the table with mine. I said, "Listen to me; I have something very important to tell you. Do I have your full attention?"

"Yes."

"I need to impress on you that God will NEVER forgive you for your mother's death!"

"What!" she interjected. "I never imagined you'd say that!"

"Well, there's a very good reason He won't. Are you listening to me? God won't forgive you for that because you're not guilty of that. He takes the issue of sin and forgiveness very seriously. Sin is what ruined the whole world. But He's also a just judge, and there's no way a newborn baby could be guilty of the death of anyone. You don't need forgiveness for this. You need to let that truth sink in. You're not guilty of your mother's death, so forgiveness can't fix it."

She had the look of a deer, caught in the headlights. Thunderstruck, is the word that came to mind. I watched her try to process this new idea. She wasn't ready to speak.

But I was. "You've carried this for a long time. This false idea has been reinforced over and over by your father's sadness. It's gone on for your whole lifetime. There are two things that cause feelings to be entrenched in our persona. The first is how young you were when it began. And the second is how often it has been reinforced in your mind. This started as early as ever happens, and has been reinforced thousands of times. You've had the maximum exposure to this lie. It may take a long time for the truth to overcome this. But the good news is God will see that it does, if you go to him in faith."

Joseph P. Smith

She reached her other hand toward me, and I covered it in mine, laying both on the table. "Would you mind if I pray for you, right here and now?"

She nodded, and I was sure that meant she wouldn't mind. I prayed that the truth would set her free. I asked for healing that only the sense of God's love could bring. I asked that the lies of the enemy of our souls would be exposed, and that she could experience the joy of salvation.

We finished our lunches in silence. As I got up, she reached out to me and thanked me. A year later, she brought her own newborn to the department to show us all the joy God was bringing to her life.

...but I obtained mercy,
because I did it ignorantly
in unbelief. 1 Timothy 1:13b

Chapter 10
The Challenge of Abortion

Hospitals can be faced with impossible ethical dilemmas. Angels do not control the hospital. Chaplains don't either. Sometimes even the executive administrators don't. Unless hospitals are part of a denominational church's ministry, government often dictates what they must do. And sometimes in the present state of things, the law clashes with Christian ethics.

I was surprised to find out that abortions could be done in our hospital. Knowing the faith position of the senior administrators, that seemed incongruent. Their churches were in the forefront of the Right to Life movement. But a little investigation showed the problem.

As a matter of "equal rights" a doctor could not be denied staff privileges in a non-church hospital because he did abortions. And if such a staff doctor applied for an operating room and its staff to do one, he had to be accommodated. No one wanted to force OR staff to assist in them, but the law required the hospital to provide staff, even when those comfortable with it couldn't be found. Fortunately, I never heard of a nurse compromised by this insanity. But the fact is it could happen.

Our hospital executives were against AOD (abortion on demand), but their hands were tied. In Grand Rapids, they perceived the majority of the public were against it. The executives didn't want the negative publicity it would bring. So the only course they could take was to make it unattractive. They required patients wanting AOD to stay in the hospital overnight, before and after the operation. I'm not sure I have all the facts here, but the message seemed to be that the law violated Christian consciences.

The serious nature of this requires that chaplains who want the light of the Gospel to penetrate the darkness of this world; have to go to some dark places, indeed. I was never tempted to refuse my services to this hospital because they did abortions.

Tales from the Toe Tag Chaplain

I thought that having the responsibility only of the Oncology Department would keep the problem away from my personal ministry area. But when I accepted the role as Director of Chaplains, this was not possible. And the fact is, abortions in hospitals were so rare, I never thought about that before accepting the directorship.

Thinking ahead of its time, our hospital had a special department for High-risk Obstetrics. And our assigned chaplain there was as godly and effective as anyone we had. She was a mother of two children, both of whom were born with severe breathing problems. The hyperbaric treatment for this was so new, that when her first was born the hospital's maintenance department rigged a HB chamber out of an old oxygen bottle just to keep her little one alive.

This wonderful female chaplain came to me with her call slip, giving a patient's name, age, room number, and the AOD admitting diagnosis. She said, "There's no way I can compassionately counsel someone who would throw away the life of a helpless baby. I'd probably scream at her."

Joseph P. Smith

She wanted to duck. Well, she could, but I couldn't. So I said I would go see the patient, but that I wanted to have lunch with the chaplain afterward and tell her what I found. It was about 9:30 in the morning. I arrived in the room to find out the procedure had already been done. The patient wasn't entirely alert due to anesthesia. But I was greeted, not by a determined woman, asserting her rights, but by a 14-year-old girl, lost in a whirl of circumstances and scared to death.

Her story caught me unprepared. Some of it didn't "add up," but here is what she told me. Six months earlier, she had been thrown out of her parents' home, and survived on the streets, eating out of garbage cans and sleeping in doorways. A 35-year-old man took her in and fed her. When he thought he had her hooked, he began to use her sexually, and when she got pregnant, threatened to throw her out again if she didn't have an abortion. Before she told him of her pregnancy, she began to imagine how cute a baby would be, and think of it as something good.

He threatened her if she told on him. She felt she didn't have any allies, so she went to a Roman Catholic social services agency. They asked her for the name of the father, and she refused to give it. She told them she wanted to join the Catholic Church, and they offered her a catechism course. They offered her help, but were not told the whole story, and so the things they offered wouldn't work. That was on Tuesday, and now it was Thursday morning.

I couldn't prevent anything, so I counseled her that even though she had no family, God was ready to accept her into His family and be a loving father to her. The presentation seemed logical to me, but either she was too groggy, or too far removed from social norms to understand my biblical metaphors. I didn't feel led to scold her. I wanted to help.

I had lunch with the chaplain and told her the story. She openly wondered why the 35-year-old wasn't arrested for statutory rape. After lunch I went to the police station and asked if they would arrest the man. They asked for his name. I didn't have it, so they called the hospital. The hospital said the records were confidential, and they were legally forbidden to disclose them. The girl was gone. The man had come to get her, and the hospital can't keep someone who wants to leave. They only asked her to sign a waiver of any medical responsibility on their part for her discharge.

Joseph P. Smith

It's a gruesome, frustrating story, but not everything has a happy ending in hospital chaplaincy. I realize that we've been called to minister in an imperfect world. Occasionally it's our turn to be the victim of its imperfection.

> Remember the prisoners,
> as though in prison with them,
> and those who are ill-treated,
> since you yourselves also are in the body.
> Hebrews 13:3

Chapter 11
Setting Captives Free
(or not)

A deputy sheriff lolled in a chair just outside the door, and enquired who I was. He allowed me past, and then closed the door, to give us some privacy. I wasn't sure I wanted privacy but upon entering, I found the patient shackled by his left ankle to the bed frame. It seemed safe enough.

Except for the shackle, the scene seemed ordinary. A patient in pajama bottoms and an open-backed gown, hooked up to a dripping IV, didn't seem so different. But then, things are often not what they seem.

"Hi Samuel*, I'm the chaplain on this floor and you're a new patient. So I stopped by to see if there was anything I could help with. For instance, I like to pray with patients, and will do so if you tell me what you want me to pray for."

"Well, Chaplain, you can see I've got myself in a fix. While I was waiting for my trial to come up, the doctor at the jail saw some things that weren't normal, and when they sent me here, they diagnosed cancer."

"Wow, that's a double whammy. You've got your own body fighting you while you fight the law."

"I guess you could say that. Actually, I don't feel too bad, and this place is better than the Kent County lockup. My trial has been put off until I get well, and who knows how long that will be. But the longer the better."

"Why do you say that?" I asked.

"My lawyer says my chances aren't too good in the trial. My ex-girl-friend is going to testify that she watched me kill her sister. And there's some truth to it."

"Is this something you want to get off your chest?"

"Well, first of all, I want to be sure you won't squeal on me. I've got enough trouble."

"If you want to confess as part of my spiritual help, my lips are sealed. I'm protected by law from revealing anything you tell me. That is, unless you're going to confess child molestation. That's something other clergy are protected from, but hospital employees aren't. We're not really hospital employees, but we're not sure how the law looks at it. So before you spill anything, I have to warn you that if it involves a child, your confession isn't safe."

He laughed. "Isn't that strange! Murder is safe, and child molestation isn't?!"

"Yeah. Whoever said the law is strange had it about right."

Tales from The Toe Tag Chaplain

"Well, to tell you the truth, I wasn't thinking about my soul when I wanted to talk to you. I am just so burnt up about the injustice. And I wasn't going to confess to the murder, but what I have to say makes me just as guilty in the eyes of the law."

"Now you have me intrigued! I can't imagine what you're talking about. But I'll treat this as an exploratory confession, and I won't tell anybody."

"Well, here's the story. My girlfriend's sister got a new car. We came to her apartment to ask if we could borrow it. Neither of us had a driver's license, so she said no. I grabbed her and held her arms behind her back, thinking my girlfriend would go after the keys, but she had a steak knife in her hand, and started stabbing her sister with it. Since we were technically going to steal the car, and auto theft is a felony, when a murder happens during the committing of a felony, all the parties to the felony are guilty of the murder."

"Whoa! You've just said a mouthful! But the thing that arouses my curiosity is that you've described the felony murder statute in terms that I would expect from a lawyer. Where did you learn that?"

I was trying to think as fast as I ever had. I wanted to get some background on this guy before we concentrated on the crime itself. Inquiry about his education seemed to be my opportunity.

He chuckled, "Nah, I'm not a lawyer. I dropped out of school as soon as I could. I just learned that on the street."

Joseph P. Smith

No one ever got into such details of the law "on the street" unless he made a career out of crime. He probably wasn't as nice a guy as he seemed.

"But you're what people call well spoken. You don't have a street accent. I'd have guessed you were educated."

"I was raised by my grandmother. She always tried to bring me up right. Took me to church every Sunday. But as I got older, I was too much for her to handle."

"Then, how is it that your ex-girlfriend can testify against you without incriminating herself?"

"Well, you see, the dirty deed took place almost three years ago. We cleaned up the place pretty well, and the cops had no suspects or motive. So I thought we were home free. Then I got a job in another town, and she didn't want to move, so I dumped her. That's when she went to the police, and told them the whole murder was my idea, and never mentioned the car. If I hadn't dumped her, I'd still be free."

"The cops just accepted her story?"

"I guess so. Anyway, I got arrested. I'm sorry I gave her my new address."

"Well, you don't seem to think you're guilty. But looking at your whole life, how do you think God will judge you?"

"I don't want to find out any time soon. The doctors say I have a good chance to beat the cancer. And Michigan doesn't have the death penalty."

He was obviously not repentant. To him, his only problem was being caught. Time might change his attitude, but there wasn't much I could do for him that day. "Do you mind if I pray for you?" I asked.

"Don't make it too long, and don't expect many amens."

My prayer asked for eternal wisdom for him, that he would see his life in terms of eternity. As requested, I kept it short, and then left.

The jail had an infirmary, and his only reason for hospitalization was to have chemotherapy, so I only saw him monthly. I tried to be alert to his admissions, since his stays were so short. We developed cordiality between us. I can't say we were friends. But he began to call me Padre, and seemed to look forward to my visits.

His spiritual inquiries were usually about irrelevant things.

"Hey, Padre, is it true that if your brother dies, you have to marry his wife?"

"You're reading the Bible. That's good, but the part you're reading won't do you much good. You should be reading about the gospel, forgiveness, and what Jesus did and can do for you."

"Ok. Padre, but humor me."

"Has your married brother died?"

"No, but it seems so crazy, I just want to know why the Bible would say that."

"Ok. I'll humor you a little. This is one of those things that can't be understood without knowing the customs and laws of the Bible times. And believe it or not, this one has to do with the inheritance of land. In our laws, when you buy a

Joseph P. Smith

piece of land, it is deeded to you and your heirs and assigns in perpetuity. That's legalese meaning the seller never has any claim against it again.

"But in the Middle East during the time this law was devised, it wasn't that way. Land belonged to the family who originally owned it, and selling it was like it would be for us to lease it until the year of jubilee. That happened every fifty years. Only males could own land, so if a man died without a male heir, the ownership of the land was in question. So the law was that if her husband's brother gave her a son, the boy would be counted as his brother's heir. This means that then the living brother couldn't inherit it."

"Boy, Padre, that's quite a setup. So it wasn't about his getting in his brother's wife's pants, but about land ownership? Sounds almost like a legit artificial insemination!"

"Yeah, sort of. But the thing you should be looking at is inheriting eternal life. This stuff is only interesting to history buffs."

"Well, it's interesting to me. You know a lot about the Bible. Maybe I ought to go to college and become a preacher."

"I think you can see you have two problems there. First, you have to lick this cancer. And then, you have to beat the rap. But even if you do both those things, before you can really become God's servant, you need to become His child. Hard as it is to beat man's law, it's a piece of cake compared to dealing with Somebody who knows everything. But that's why Jesus is like our lawyer. He has this defense all worked out. As soon as we're accused, He's going to say, 'I died in this fellow's place. The penalty is paid. It's not fair to ask for the payment twice.'

"But that's only if He's your advocate. That's another word for lawyer. He becomes our advocate when we trust Him as our Savior."

"We'll see, Padre, we'll see."

It was getting harder to get through the shell of his ego. He was so proud of being able to meet his own needs by his wits, that he couldn't accept help outside his control. No matter how I tried, I could not get through his defenses.

But the cancer got him before the law could. He spent his last seven days on earth in our department, and I prayed with him every day.

In his weakened condition, he finally asked me for something.

"I know I'm dying. I want you to promise me that when I'm gone, you'll tell the cops that I didn't do it. I want that lousy woman to suffer."

"I probably won't do that. You're motive is revenge, and I might be jeopardizing the clergy penitent legal protection."

"No, Padre, the privacy law doesn't apply to the dead. And it doesn't matter what my motives are. You should be concerned about justice. It's not a favor to me. It's just setting things straight."

"Ok. I've never heard that interpretation of the shield law, but you're more of a lawyer than I am. I'll check and see if you're right. And if you are, I'll tell the cops what you told me."

Joseph P. Smith

"And there is one favor to me. Would you go to my grandmother and tell her I love her, and that I never wanted to murder that girl. The old gal did her best for me, and I want her to know it did some good."

"Ok. The same condition applies. If as you say, it won't hurt the shield law, I'll be glad to."

"His face relaxed. He held my hand while I prayed, but didn't open his eyes afterward."

He died sometime in that night and I never saw him again. But a lawyer friend told me I wouldn't jeopardize the shield law, and I went to the Grand Rapids Detective Bureau with the story. They said the woman had passed a lie detector test, so they weren't interested in my input. But his grandmother thanked me through her tears.

> ... reprove, rebuke, exhort,
> with great patience
> and instruction.
> 2 Timothy 4:2b

Chapter 12
Another Job Description Adjustment

I raised my head from the paperwork I was doing at the charting station, to hear a loud argument coming down the hall. It was most uncharacteristic for our department.

"What's that?" I asked no one in particular.

"It's 407a," a nurse responded.

"What's he so upset about," I asked.

"He has testicular cancer. It's one of our most treatable cancers. But the protocol requires we do blood tests the day before chemo, and we were letting him do it all as an outpatient. The problem is, he would come in for the tests, and we'd study them against the progress in the Sloan-Kettering protocols, work up a plan, and then he'd just decide to go fishing and not come in for his treatment. This has gone on for months. So we told him. No more

Joseph P. Smith

outpatient. He'd have to stay in house between the tests and the treatment. He thought we didn't mean it, but when he came in for his tests we admitted him, and he's not happy."

I said, "I'm hearing obscenities. If I can hear them way down here, what about the people in the rooms down there?"

"Yeah, that's the problem. The lady in 405 says she shouldn't have to put up with this stuff. She's more in need of treatment than he is, but she's threatening to go home."

The head nurse interrupted. "Maybe, Chaplain, you ought to go down there and give it to that kid. He needs to be told off."

"That's not in my job description," I replied.

It was lunch time, and that was a good excuse to get out of there. So I headed for the cafeteria. But all the time, I was thinking about what a quandary this was for the hospital staff. I decided to do a little investigation. So I began asking his caregivers what they knew about him. They told me he was the only child of a single mother, and that he completely dominated her. Several of them commented on how odd their relationship was. Several said he acted like his mother's parent. One implied that the relationship was kinkier than that.

I didn't want to uncork a bottle I couldn't stop up later, so I just let that one die in the dust. But I wondered if he had ever had an authority figure in his life. So I decided to be one.

Tales from The Toe Tag Chaplain

I entered the room empty handed, because I wanted him to know that what I was about to do was my only mission there.

"Son," I said in a normal tone but with all the firmness I could muster. "I'm the chaplain of this department, but I have an unusual purpose today. You've missed three months of treatment by your shenanigans, and the staff here is ready to throw you out again. When you were diagnosed, we thought we had about a 90% chance of curing you. But that cancer in your body doesn't care about making things the way you want them. You can't bully it, it's never going to be afraid of you. It's been growing so that those chances are less than 50/50 now.

"This behavior has to stop! You may have condemned yourself to die of this disease, but when you did, you condemned us to watch it! And we don't like that one bit. But we have an easy out, here. We can just send you home with no treatment and then we won't have to put up with this. There are other patients who need us and want to go home so they don't have to put up with it either. We're sick of this crap, and we don't want any more."

His roommate, well into his 70s and with painful lung cancer, was struggling to sit up. When I finished, he struggled to breathe so he could speak. He said, "Son, listen to him. This guy is giving you the straight scoop."

It's funny. I never talked to that guy, but I remember his name. Fred's short speech won the battle. My patient quieted, even though scowling.

Joseph P. Smith

But now, I wondered if I had burned the bridges that could build a spiritually profitable relationship. I was in uncharted waters for sure.

When I got to him the next day, it was like the day before had never happened. He was hooked up to his IV, the top of the bed cranked up so he was almost sitting. That's unusual when you're getting chemo.

Fred was quietly snoring. My patient looked bored.

"Do you have anything to read?" I asked. "I can get today's paper for you."

"Yeah, that would be nice. I wish I had a radio so I could listen to the ball game. But with a paper, I'll be able to get yesterday's results."

Television added $2.50 a day to the bill, and I guess he didn't have it. But patients were allowed to have their own small radio on the night stand.

"I'll have to go to the outside door of the hospital where the newspaper machines are, so I'll be gone a few minutes. In the meantime, maybe you'd like to look over the little devotional booklet we bring." I handed him the latest *Daily Bread* and headed for the door.

When I got back, he thanked me for the paper, but didn't open it. I couldn't see the booklet anywhere. I had no idea of how to follow-up, so I just left.

Tales from The Toe Tag Chaplain

This was the beginning of about a year of our testy relationship. I got to meet his mother and we talked in a normal way, but her relationship with her son was odd, indeed.

Her pet names for him were usually reserved for lovers. Every sentence contained at least one *sweety* or *honey* or *lover*. Her kisses didn't seem motherly.

One day she was sitting in the family room instead of his room. "Does the hospital have a chapel?" she asked.

"Yes," I said. "If you want to see it, I'm on my way there. You can come with me."

Little did I know what I was in for. I showed her to a pew, and then proceeded into the Sacristy - a U-shaped room surrounding the pulpit and altar of the chapel. There was only one door, facing the left side of the nave, or congregational seating. Just inside the door were some open closet fixtures, as it was designed so clergy could change into liturgical robes there prior to services. At the far end of the U was a large cupboard, where we kept literature and supplies. I was there to get a pocketful of devotional booklets, and didn't notice the woman until I felt her pressing into my backside.

I turned to defend myself, and said, "You're not supposed to be in here! What are you doing?"

"They won't let me see my boy," she said. "I miss him so much; I just wanted a little comfort."

Joseph P. Smith

"I guess what you want could be called comfort," I said. "But I'm a servant of God, and I don't provide that kind. Now you get out of here, and let me alone."

I pushed her toward the door, but she had locked it. If there was any doubt about her intentions, that erased it. I had used my key to get in, but unfortunately left it unlocked behind me, thinking I'd only be a moment. I unlocked the door to let us both out, and then pushed past her, returning to my job.

Back at the nurses' station, I asked, "Is it true that you won't let the boy's mother visit him?"

"That's right. She can see him for short visits if there's a staff person in the room. But we think she's been supplying him with some sort of drugs. So we won't let her near the bed, and she can't be in there alone."

I never expected to see this in our hospital.

"What is it with that woman? She tried to grope me in the Sacristy of the Chapel."

"Her doctor supplies her with amphetamines for weight control, and it makes her hyper sexual," was the reply. Even in that day, that treatment was frowned on, but not yet cause for discipline. Still a few doctors used them. I'd have to treat her like she had the plague.

Her visits to her son got more infrequent. And my visits were getting longer. Our conversations never got to spiritual things. Usually they flitted from one subject to another until he got to something he could boast about. And eventually, he was flat on his back, hooked up to a morphine drip for pain.

I had discovered he couldn't read. It happened one day when he was looking over the baseball standings and confused New York with St. Louis. A lot of good the devotional booklets were doing him! But I didn't let on I knew.

One day he was lying on his back, holding a sharp pencil in one hand and a piece of paper with the *Daily Bread* behind it in the other. He was obviously drawing something in that awkward position.

"Can I see?" I asked.

"Sure."

It was a pencil portrait of a very pretty night nurse. It would have been remarkable under any circumstances, but executed while flat on his back, it was indeed marvelous.

"I didn't know you were such an artist," I said.

"Oh yeah, give me the right size piece of paper and a sharp pencil, and I'll draw you a dollar bill so good you can buy cigarettes with it in the machine down the hall!

"Well, I might just take you up on that. I don't want to buy cigarettes with it, but a charity where I'm on the board wants to make a slide show on how carefully they use money. It's going to be called *George Washington Never Slept Here*. But after we thought up the idea, we found it was illegal to take pictures of real money. We could really use a drawing like that.

He agreed to do it. I got him a piece of paper of the right proportions but a little larger than a dollar, and about six sharp pencils.

When I saw him a week later, he showed me his masterpiece. George was gorgeous, but United had no "t" and Dollar had only one "l."

I didn't point that out, but simply praised him. He could be justly proud, and we'd figure out a way to use the drawing. I just kept pointing out the good features, and taking time to rave a little. Every compliment made his chest swell a little.

"You've known you had this talent for a long time. Have you ever wondered why God would be so good to you when you usually ignore Him?" I asked.

It took a little time for him to catch up with this switch in the conversation, and that allowed me to go on.

"Take you, for instance. You play the part of a tough guy, independent, doing what you want. But you have the sensitive soul of an artist. You need to put on a rough exterior, but all it does is cover up what's really valuable in you, a talent that's very exceptional.

"You care a lot that people won't get the idea you have any weakness, but inside you're always putting up a front. The idea that God has an investment in you He wants to develop, scares you.

Tales from The Toe Tag Chaplain

But in a way, you're just like the fake dollar you gave me. Maybe even like this real one."

I took a dollar bill out of my wallet.

"You see, they're both just a piece of paper. In themselves, they're only good to light a fire. But we say that real one is worth a dollar. Why? Because someone else also thinks it's worth a dollar and will trade a dollar's worth of stuff for it. We call that attributed value. We attribute worth to it by what we'll give for it.

"How does God see you? Actually, you're a pain in the neck! But in spite of that, you're a being created in His image, damaged and some would say with the image of God destroyed in you. But God chooses to love you, and he proved that by what He gave for you."

"What's that?"

"All your bad behavior, just like my own bad behavior, deserves to be punished in a place Jesus called hell. But He took the punishment we deserve so God could accept us without any injustice. He paid the entire penalty for your sin. He wants you to accept His death as if it were your own, and to allow Him to live in you.

"See, that's your attributed value. God gave His precious Son for you. You're not really worth it, but He wants to make you worth it. But of course, you can choose to throw it away by ignoring His love and just toughing it out on your own."

Joseph P. Smith

He finally spoke, "I know what you're talking about. I've heard it on the free channel on Sunday. I have a lot to think about. We can talk more later."

Neither of us knew that he had just two more weeks to live. I never learned what he did with God's offer of salvation. But I'm glad he heard it clearly. And it all started as strangely as a chaplain could imagine—with loud ranting and cussing in a hospital room.

> ...knowing this, that our old self
> was crucified with Him,
> in order that our body of sin
> might be done away with,
> so that we would no longer
> be slaves to sin;...
> Romans 6:6

Chapter 13
Victory Over Self

"Are you the Chaplain? Why don't you ever come to see me?"

The voice was loud enough to catch my attention as I walked past the door. But there was something of struggle in its sound that let me know it came with great effort. I backed up and stood in the doorway.

"Yes. I'm Chaplain Smith, assigned to this unit. But the reason I haven't stopped is that you have evident pastoral care. I've seen your pastor, and he visits often. We know your church from the intake information you gave. It's actually one of the churches that support our chaplaincy. I'd love to visit with you, but I don't want to interfere with an ongoing pastor/parishioner relationship."

"You wouldn't be interfering. I just see you walking by with your Bible in hand. And knowing we had a chaplain here, I wondered if you were him."

Joseph P. Smith

"Do you really want me to visit you?" I asked.

"Yes. When I'm at home, I have neighbors from the church that I go to for prayer. Here, I'm kind of cut off from them. We can talk on the phone, but I miss the family feeling they give me when we're together. And besides, I need all the prayer I can get! So that you can pray for me at other times, my name is Ginny*."

I could understand Ginny's need for prayer. Under the bed, out of her sight, but plain to the visitor was a large jar with hoses in the lid, obviously a vacuum set up, drawing the ugliest grayish-brown stuff from somewhere in her body. I could assume the drains were in her lung area, because of the sound of her voice.

"Are things not going well?" I enquired.

"The doctors seem satisfied with my progress. But all this equipment means that I can't move very much, and I can't get comfortable. There's constant low grade pain, and I get stiff."

"I see. With acute pain, we bear it because it doesn't last long. But chronic pain means that the strong addicting pain medications aren't appropriate. They're only for short term pain."

"You do understand. I feel ashamed for complaining about pain, because it isn't very severe. It's just that it's always there, from the minute I wake up, until I fall asleep, exhausted. Pain like this seems to underline how lonely I am here. It's easier to forget it if I have someone to talk with."

TALES FROM THE TOE TAG CHAPLAIN

It was humbling to think about how often my efforts had all the benefit of an aspirin.

"Of course, I'll be glad to visit. And I love to pray with patients. Most of the time, I don't get to pray with them, only for them. What should we pray about?"

"We can pray for my family. I have two little girls and a blind husband. He has his hands full right now. And we can pray for this treatment. I'm really tired of this trial. I guess it's my cross to bear, but I want to get it over with."

"Ok. Let's pray."

I always start my prayers with thanksgiving. So I thanked God for this new friend and that someone as unworthy as I could help her. I quoted the scripture, "After you have suffered for a little while, the God of all grace, who called you to His eternal glory in Christ, will Himself perfect, confirm, strengthen and establish you."

I prayed for an end to her suffering, and that she would be able as never before to serve in her vital role in the family. She prayed for her husband and children by name, thanked God for her doctors and hospital staff, and for the assurance that she was God's child, and that He would care for her, no matter what happened.

I took her hand, promised to never pass by her door again without checking in, and went on my rounds.

Joseph P. Smith

So began a regular relationship for several months, while she struggled with her pain and family concerns. Her condition wasn't getting worse, but there didn't seem to be much progress either.

Then one day, she gave me a positive announcement.

"Chaplain Smith, I've really come to the conclusion that God is going to heal me!"

"Ginny, you sound positive of that. Tell me how you came to that conclusion."

"Well, if it was all about me, God's will might not be to cure this cancer. But my kids need me. And my husband is a patent attorney. He works out of our home, and I usually read all his correspondence to him. I can't imagine how he gets along without me. But I've been praying for God will meet the needs of him and my little girls, and they need me. So I'm sure God is going to heal me."

"I've heard a number of people say they believed God was going to heal them. But I've never heard such a clear rationale for it as this one. I think we should begin to pray in faith for His hand to heal."

And sure enough, as we began to pray that way, her condition improved. First the tubes came out. Then she began walking with a nurse holding on, and then, as much as she wanted, alone. She thanked God during our prayer times for the ability to care for her own bodily needs, without asking staff to help.

TALES FROM THE TOE TAG CHAPLAIN

Her discharge wasn't announced to me, and it came late in the day, after I had gone home. But she left a wonderful little "Thank You" card for me. She must have brought a box full of them, because other members of the staff got them also.

I was sorry we had not been able to say goodbye face-to-face, but was thankful for her freedom from pain, and her return to her family. However, I missed my prayer partner.

Then her recovery went sour. She was admitted again, and her health was in a downward spiral. What had seemed an answer to prayer was turning into something else. One of the casualties of her illness was her participation in our prayer times. She'd hold my hand while we prayed, give a tight squeeze where an amen should come, but she couldn't bring herself to speak aloud to God.

I got to meet her husband. Edgar* was a remarkable guy, gifted with a wonderful memory that enabled him to keep many details about patent applications in order, so that he could argue for the unique and ground breaking qualities of an invention.

He began to visit her regularly at the same time most afternoons. Someone from their church had volunteered to drive him. Often I would time my visits to be there to include him in our prayer times. Of course, my visits were short, and I left plenty of time for them to be alone.

One day, I got there before he did. And Ginny had a new announcement for me.

Joseph P. Smith

"Chaplain Smith, do you remember when I told you that God was going to heal me because my husband and kids needed me? Well, it occurred to me this morning that they need somebody, but it might not be me!"

How do you respond to that! I said, "Wow! That's a mouthful! I'm having a hard time processing the implications." *It was better to be honest.*

Just then, Edgar walked into the room. "Hi, honey. You're looking good."

Of course he was joking. He tried hard to get Ginny to cheer up.

"Oh Edgar, this is no time for your lame jokes," she snapped.

I said, "Ginny, it's time for me to leave you two alone. We'll see each other again.

But Edgar followed me out in the hall. "What's the matter with her?" he asked.

Edgar, I think I know, but I don't know any way to tell you. I'm sure she loves you and the kids. That's the most important thing. Her mind is trying to find a logical way to explain what is happening, so she's dealing with deep feelings. Just keep on loving her. It will all come out in the end."

But inwardly I was thinking *she's already jealous of whoever is to be her replacement. And we're not even sure she will be replaced!*

Tales from the Toe Tag Chaplain

One day, Ginny was thinking about her college roommate who had never married, and worked as a high school history teacher. It was June and school was out, so she invited Janice* to visit her when Edger would be there.

They got along famously, and then Janice offered to drive Edgar to the hospital, and stopping at their home, got to meet their daughters.

Later, Janice was telling me how much the daughters missed their mother. I told her that our department sometimes relaxed the visitor's rules in cases like this, and I worked it out with the powers that be. The next visit she brought the whole family.

There were several more of these family visits, before the medical staff announced that they weren't going to try any more to cure her, but only to manage the symptoms.

Those were tear-filled days. Every visit might be a goodbye.

Her primary care oncologist was a brilliant scientist, but not given to empathy. He had never expressed feelings to any of this family. And an unusual fact was that Edgar, Ginny and he, had all attended the same kindergarten. Unknown to me, they had an uncomplimentary nickname for him.

I asked Ginny if there was anything special she wanted in her care.

She said, "Yes. I don't want to die in the hospital. I want to have all the time I can at home with them."

Joseph P. Smith

The head nurse was doubtful it could be done. The social worker, who plays a big part in discharge plans, noticed that she would need around-the-clock nursing care. I called her pastor to tell him of the special need. He arranged with five retired nurses in his congregation to volunteer to stay with her. Grand Rapids Hospice, in its infancy showed us how to get the legalities done.

The plan was for Ginny to go home on a Wednesday afternoon. As the nurses were getting her ready for the wheel chair ride to the car, her doctor intruded, "You can't do this. There's a test I want to run!"

"Get lost, Tubby," Edgar* said using the uncomplimentary nickname. "She doesn't need your test. She's ready for her finals."

They wheeled her out of the department, and I never saw her again. The funeral announcement was in the Sunday paper.

But I wasn't surprised to see a wedding announcement six months later. Edgar and Janice were to be married. I hadn't gone to the funeral, but I went to the wedding.

Ginny is one of my heroes. Her unselfish love for her husband and children overcame a selfish affection. She was permanently healed, and actively helped God meet the needs of her family.

> "I will lead the blind by a way
> they do not know,
> In paths they do not know
> I will guide them."
> Isaiah 42:16

Chapter 14
Baseball Babies

What usually woke me at night was the beeper. Since I had taken on the Directorship of our Hospital Chaplaincy Service, I was on emergency call to all six hospitals we served. But I had just gotten into a deep sleep. So it took a little time to realize that it was the telephone.

Wondering who would call at this hour, I tried to shake myself awake so as to get my brain in gear before I said anything.

"Hello?"

"Hello, Chaplain Smith. I'm the head nurse of the O. B. Department of Xxxxxx hospital. We have an emergency here that needs some spiritual input from a protestant chaplain. It could take a long time to explain the situation and we need to hurry, so would you trust me and come right down?"

It wasn't one of our hospitals. It was a fine Catholic hospital that provided their own pastoral care. I knew the head of the department. He was an excellent hospital care giver. I assumed that he had protestant chaplains on staff, so I was puzzled by the call. But I responded that I would come right down. It was nine miles away, and at this time there would be little traffic, so I said I'd be there in about twenty minutes.

"One of our nurses will meet you at the emergency room door. There's an emergency parking spot there, and I'll have the ER people ready to put a permit under your windshield wiper. Thanks so much for your willingness to come!"

"Be right there," and I hung up, reaching for my clothes.

So much that was happening seemed off the wall. But the communication from the nurse demonstrated that she was detail oriented. She had correctly assumed that I didn't know where their obstetrics department was. And she thought through my parking need. So I had to assume she knew what she was doing.

It was a good thing the nurse met me. Hospitals are often added on to like a game of dominos. I get this irrational feeling that hospital architects warm up on the Minotaur's labyrinth. Although well marked, the way to O.B. wasn't easy to follow.

The room was pleasant but crowded. The patient was hooked up to an IV, and there were two nurses hovering over her. In one chair was a woman who looked enough like the patient to be her sister. The other held a young man, who I assumed was the patient's husband.

"Thanks for coming Pastor," said the voice I'd heard on the phone. "Mrs. Jones* here is pregnant with twins. Her husband wasn't at home when her labor started, so her sister brought her in. She's not very close to full term, so with her permission, the doctor started treatment to stop the labor. But when her husband got here, he told us to stop the treatment. We think we can keep these babies in their mother, and that's where they need to be. We can't risk stopping the treatment."

There were a couple of things I had to consider. First of all, a husband does not own his wife's body. The only one who can order either starting or stopping treatment is the patient. And she had given permission for treatment to start. I was sure she had signed a paper we call "informed consent to treat." Only she could revoke it.

But just looking at the mother-to-be showed the other side of the problem. She was not at all comfortable with stopping treatment, but she also wanted to obey her husband. It seemed to be more than ordinary marital consensus. He clearly dominated her.

I first turned to the husband. "Tell me your thinking about stopping the treatment," I asked.

"If God wants those babies to come now, that's His will, and I believe in submission to the will of God."

"That's not a statement from someone who is casual about God. It sounds to me like you go to church."

"I was brought up in a Full Gospel Church, and we were married there. We attend every Sunday and Wednesday. We are taught to present our bodies a living sacrifice, holy, acceptable unto God, which is our reasonable service. And be not conformed to this world: but be transformed by the renewing of our minds, that we may prove what is that good, and acceptable, and perfect, will of God."

Joseph P. Smith

Except for the grammatical changes, it came right out of the King James Version.

I said, "I'm interested in how you apply those verses. Tell me, you went to school, right?

"Of course."

"Well, when you entered kindergarten, weren't you given some shots, and a smallpox vaccination?"

"So what?"

"Well, it might have been God's will for you to get smallpox. Why did you medically prevent it, but you don't want to prevent this?"

"Ah, you're just trying to trick me. Are you really a protestant chaplain? I told them I didn't want one from this hospital!"

That explained the call. And confirmed to me that this head nurse knew her way around. But it left me wondering.

"Of course I'm not on the staff of this hospital. But if you wanted to be sure of where the advice was coming from, why didn't you call your own pastor?"

"I didn't want to bother him. You guys are paid to come here at night."

In this case, it wasn't true, but I didn't want to argue. He wasn't making sense to me.

"Let's stick to the subject. You must have a doctor, right?

"Well, yeah."

"Why didn't you call him?"

Tales from The Toe Tag Chaplain

"I've been on medical disability for over a year because I hurt my knee at work. Money is tight at our house, And with twins coming, I can't afford to run up more medical bills."

"Oh, I assumed you were at work or something. Where were you when the labor started?"

"At a ball game. It's one of the city leagues."

"So you were watching a game. Why wasn't your wife with you?"

"She doesn't like sitting alone in the bleachers."

"Why don't you sit with her?"

"I'm playing second base."

So much for the disability. I was really getting to dislike this guy.

"Are you sure you still want the treatment to stop? And how about you Mrs. Jones? What do you want?"

"I'm scared. But the Bible says, 'Wives, submit to your husbands.'"

The spiritual counsel wasn't getting us anywhere. I had a new idea of how to deal with this.

"How far along are you?" I asked.

"Twenty-six weeks."

"Ok. In the interest of full disclosure, I need to tell you what's ahead. In all likelihood, if you stop treatment, the babies will be born tonight. They're probably going to be born alive. But they are going to be life threatened from the beginning. This hospital doesn't have a neo-natal unit, so they'll be transferred to the hospital where I work. Babies have survived that are even more premature. But they won't be able to go home for somewhere between six to twelve weeks. The daily rate for neo-natal care is a thousand dollars a day for each of them. You'll come out of this owing about sixty to eighty thousand dollars. Do you have insurance that will cover that? And that's not the end of it. They could have lung damage that will handicap them for life. And you'll be on the hook for them until they're adults. You're headed for a lifetime of poverty!"

I had no idea whether this was all true, but I tried to look and sound like it did. Theology wasn't what this guy needed, he needed a jolt.

"Let's leave this couple alone for a few minutes so they can make up their minds." As I was talking I gently took the sister by the arm, nodded to the nurses to come too, and started out.

It couldn't have been more than thirty seconds after we closed the door when the husband came out, and said, "You can keep the IV in."

We went back inside and I prayed for the success of the treatment, for God to reveal His will, and that the rest of the pregnancy would be uneventful.

Six weeks later I saw the birth announcement in the paper.

All the peoples of the earth
are regarded as nothing.
He does as he pleases
with the powers of heaven
and the peoples of the earth.
No one can hold back his hand
or say to him: "What have you done?"

Chapter 15
An Identity Crisis

"Why does the Accounting Department want to see me?"

It was our usual practice to check for new admissions at the information center upon entering the hospital. But this pink summons was unusual, indeed!

"We don't know any more than you," the telephone operator said. "We just took the call. You have all the information we got right there."

Could we be liable for any costs I didn't know about? We weren't paid by the hospital, but they gave us free parking and access to the cafeteria. *Was there something I missed?*

My mind was searching for an answer so I wasn't prepared for the reality.

"Come in and sit down, Reverend Smith," the head of accounting said. "We're going to ask you to do something for us. It's not something in our contractual relationship, but I think you're the right one to ask."

A bit relieved that it wasn't going to strain out tight budget I replied, "Ok. How can we help?"

"Late yesterday we admitted a patient to your oncology department. It now appears that the name she gave us is fictitious, and her address is in the middle of the Grand River. We can start a file using this false data, but we'd rather get it straight. She seems like a nice lady. We don't suspect fraud, but we can't imagine her reason for doing that.

"Ordinarily we'd just send a clerk to straighten it out. But something tells us there's more here than meets the eye. We want someone with a lot of tact to talk to her. Please see if you can find out what's going on."

I was flattered that they thought I was tactful. I also wanted to show that we were willing partners with the hospital. So, though a little unsure of myself, I said, "Thanks for thinking of us. We want to be helpful. A chaplain with a Bible is a lot less threatening than a bookkeeper with a clipboard. I'll give it my best shot."

But how would I do this? All my training and experience in conversational ministry never had this in mind. I'd have to wing it. And my suspicion was that I needed to be kind, but direct.

I started at the unit desk. "I see the person in 413b was admitted yesterday with a diagnosis of a suspected tumor. Has she been worked up yet? I've been asked by the hospital to get some rather personal information about her, and I need to know how far along we are."

"Let's see, we know that she has cervical cancer, and she was informed this morning. Her doctor will be in later this morning to discuss treatment with her."

I wasn't sure why I had asked for this. I just wanted to be sure not to be surprised by anything I found. But the answer I got was on the edge of violating her privacy. We were not technically employees of the hospital, so we usually don't get medical information. That's the disadvantage of not being on staff. You don't get to understand the whole picture.

My plan was forming. I'd begin the visit in the usual way for new patients, but add in what we knew about her. If she wanted to disclose the reason for her deception or not, that was up to her. But I usually used their name in introducing myself, and using her false name might not be a good idea.

The room was bright, the venetian blinds pulled up, but there were no cards or flowers. My patient wasn't in a hospital gown, but flannel pajamas with a small floral pattern. She was nice looking, without make-up, but with a neat hair-do that she had obviously worked on since she awoke.

"Hi there. I'm Chaplain Smith, and I call on all new patients whose admission data doesn't show evidence of pastoral care, to see if there's some way I can help. You didn't list a church, right?"

Joseph P. Smith

"That's right."

"Well I'm here to pray with you or do anything else I can to help. And I see the medical people have already been busy on your case. You should have a treatment plan later this morning."

She didn't respond but looked hopeful.

"There's just one thing. We have reason to believe that the name you gave is fictitious, and the address you gave is underwater, in the Grand River. You look like an honest person, so we think you're hiding your hospital admission from somebody. We want you to know that we keep that information confidential, and no one will know this if you don't want them to. But it puts us in a difficult position to have false data."

She looked disconsolate. "I'm sorry; I didn't want to cause trouble. Before I came here, I took all the money out of my personal savings account so I could pay you. But you're right. There's someone I don't want to know I'm here."

"Maybe we can help you keep your secret. Who is it you don't want to know?"

"My husband."

"Is there a strain in your marriage?"

"No."

"Can you help me understand why?"

"He's a pastor."

"That is a surprise to me. What does that have to do with your need for secrecy?"

"Our church is in a very small denomination. What we believe isn't very common. You see, our church teaches that all sickness is the result of sin. When the sin is confessed and you are forgiven, the illness goes away. But I started having these symptoms six weeks ago. I confessed every sin I possibly committed unknowingly, but the symptoms won't go away. I don't know where they are coming from, but I wanted to see what the doctors thought. We're not supposed to do that, and I don't want my husband to know."

"Well, your admission won't be in the paper, and we won't notify him. That's not the problem. Have you been told what the doctors think?"

I wasn't supposed to know, so I needed her to tell me.

"They say I have cervical cancer. I know what a cervix is, but I don't know how they know that."

"I don't know what tests they've run, but they don't make that diagnosis without good evidence. Have they given you a 'female' examination?"

"Yes."

"Then they can probably see the tumor, and they've probably taken a small tissue sample called a biopsy. It takes a while for the full tests on that to come back, but they take a quick look at part of that tissue they call a frozen section. It's not a perfect test, but it's probably right. They won't wait for the full study to come back before they start a treatment plan. Delaying it could be dangerous."

"But I need to go home."

"I guess I can understand that. Your husband must be crazy, wondering where you are."

"No. He thinks I'm at my sister's. I've sworn her to secrecy."

"Isn't lying like that a sin? But you don't think that's the cause of your symptoms."

"No. Because my lies were not meant to hurt him. And besides, I've confessed them and been forgiven."

In the back of my mind I was discouraged by how many people think sin, confession, and forgiveness is like a checker game, and the big issue is who has the next move. But I didn't want to get into all that with her.

"Just to get things straight, do you think your illness is caused by some sin in your life?"

"If it is, I don't know what!"

"I want to be frank. I don't share this concept. I'm not here to alienate you from your church, or your husband, but I'm beginning to get the idea that you're beginning to doubt it, too. And in the spirit of being completely honest, what hospitals call full disclosure, any spiritual advice I give you may be contradictory with your church's views. In fact, I can assure you that it will be. I don't want to violate your conscience, so I need to know, are you sure that sin is causing your illness?"

"No, I'm not sure."

"Well, let me tell you what everybody here thinks. Whether it comes from some inherited trait, or is caused by something that is physical in your environment, some cells in your body have begun a process of reproducing themselves in a useless and immature way. This over production of malignant cells has created a tumor, a growth in your body that will make awful demands on your bodily system. That will mean you don't have enough stuff in you that the good cells need to survive. And when that happens, you will die a rather unkind death, looking like you're starving, with normal processes blocked, and probably with pain. It's not pretty, and we don't like to see it. I don't know how far this has gone. I don't know if there are tumors that have spread to other systems. But the sooner we start to work on it, and the quicker we start destroying those bad cells, either with surgery, or radiation or chemotherapy, the better your chances are. You're facing something that to you is unusual. But to us, it's an everyday event. We deal with it all the time, and the results of treating or not treating are absolutely predictable."

A voice came from the doorway. "Chaplain, you're not supposed to give medical advice!"

It was her doctor.

"Sorry doctor. I just thought she also needed to hear it from someone in the faith community. I guess I was out of line."

"It's alright, chaplain. I wish I could have recorded it. It's exactly what I was going to say."

Whew! In a day when all kinds of boundaries were crossed, we were still on the same team.

"Ok doctor. Just understand that today; what we're telling her intensely violates everything she has believed in her adult life. She has to choose what to believe. Be gentle with her. I've come to admire and respect her. But she's a sensitive soul. Don't run over her. I'll get out of here and let the real professionals take over."

"You've behaved professionally yourself, Chaplain. I didn't really mean to scold you. But I was upholding an important rule."

"And I respect the rule. But there are times...."

I couldn't finish the sentence. I said my goodbyes and left.

Later in the afternoon, I visited again, asked her to tell me how she wanted me to pray, and we each prayed.

But sometime that evening, and I have no idea how, her husband found her. When I got back to the room in the morning, the door was closed. I knocked, waited, and peeked through a crack.

TALES FROM THE TOE TAG CHAPLAIN

"Chaplain Smith, this is my husband. We need a little privacy. Do you mind?"

"Of course not."

I closed the door, wondering how this would all come out. I only saw them one more time, that afternoon, signing the releases so she could go home.

"Are you Ok?" I asked.

"We found the sin that was causing the trouble."

"And what was that?"

"It was the sin of doubting God."

You can't win them all. I just wished the stakes weren't so high.

*Many will say to Me on that day, 'Lord, Lord,
did we not prophesy in Your name,
and in Your name cast out demons,
and in Your name perform many miracles?'
Matthew 7:22*

Chapter 16
Attempted Exorcism

I had only visited this patient once, because although she hadn't named a church on her intake data, she informed me that she had one, in a small town outside our city. She was clear that she trusted Jesus Christ as her Savior. And her pastor didn't seem to mind the distance, and visited her regularly. But things changed when she had a stroke in hospital.

The visible effect of the stroke was a total inability to communicate. She could talk. She used real words. But they tumbled out like they were being discharged from a well shaken salt cellar. They made no sense at all.

On her pastor's next visit, he was surprised at this change. He wondered if this was demon possession.

A nurse tried to explain that it was aphasia. It happens when the brain loses the connection between things and their symbols. This actually means things and their words, for practical understanding. The words are still all in the brain.

Tales from The Toe Tag Chaplain

They're just no longer connected to the things they represent.

This can be total, and when it is it is called aphasia. Or it can be partial, in which case it is called dysphasia. It can be only about hearing, called receptive aphasia, or about speaking, called expressive aphasia. When it is both, it's called global aphasia.

We didn't usually study diseases and their symptoms so much. But our ministry is accomplished through communication, and we need to know as much as possible so that ministry can be appropriate.

Another oddity is that we didn't learn about aphasia from doctors, but from speech therapists. The one on call to our floor was amazing. She could imitate different speech patterns from different dysfunctions. Her imitation of aphasia was just like this patient.

Expressive aphasia is easy to spot. It's harder to be sure about receptive aphasia. The person may actually hear and in some ways understand rational talk, but can't express his understanding. Diagnosis of expressive aphasia usually comes in less than an hour. Whether it is also receptive can take weeks. In the meantime, if it's not global, it is important that you talk to the person slowly and normally. The only result you might see is a greater calmness in the patient.

Her pastor was convinced she was possessed. How else could a calm person go from serenity to raving in such a short time? I got an appointment for him with the speech therapist, hoping she could convince him that this was the result of a stroke. It was to no avail.

When I tried to convince him, he said, "You just don't believe in demon possession!"

"Yes, I do. Jesus acknowledged it and I believe Him explicitly."

"How many cases of demon possession have you seen?"

"Well, I'm not sure I've ever seen it."

"See. I said you didn't believe in it. I've seen dozens of cases."

I wanted to respond that if he always called aphasia demon possession, I could understand that. But I bit my tongue and stood mute.

One day her nurse came to me to ask for help. "Her Pastor's with her and he's shouting at her."

Knowing how touchy a subject this was, rather than go myself I called hospital security.

"Is he touching her?"

"I don't think so."

"Is there any evidence that he is hurting her?"

"What evidence could there be?"

Tales from The Toe Tag Chaplain

"Is she complaining?"

"She can't make herself understood at all! How would anybody know?"

"If anyone else is complaining about the shouting, we can insist he keep it quiet. Otherwise, he's her pastor. We have that in writing. If she doesn't complain, there's nothing that can be done."

"Have you ever had a legal opinion on that, or is this just your take."

"Our lawyers have dealt with a dozen cases like this. Their position is that as long as no one complains, or is likely to complain, we can't do anything. In fact, they say if we put a stop to it, we could be violating her freedom of religion."

It seemed crazy, this dilemma. It pained me to think that a sweet old lady could spend the last days of her life being yelled at. I couldn't get it out of my mind.

At chaplains' prayer meeting, I mentioned this to the others. Some were especially touched with the problem. We prayed that somehow she would be spared this treatment, and have peace.

I decided to make an early morning call on her. The room door was closed, but I quietly edged in, all the while praying I'd find some way to help her. The patient was flat on her back, a slim woman who hadn't wiggled in her sleep. The covers formed a half tube over her body, and came up to her throat, but didn't cover her shoulders. Her arms were on top of the bed covers, her hands palm up, eyes closed.

I touched one hand lightly to see if she was sleeping.

It was stone cold!

I couldn't help thinking in triumph: God has already answered our prayers. Sshe already knows her pastor is a mistaken!

> "Therefore I say to you, any sin and blasphemy shall be forgiven people, but blasphemy against the Spirit shall not be forgiven.
> Matthew 12:31

Chapter 17
Unpardonable Sin

"The Lord's my shepherd, I'll not want. He makes me down to lie in pastures green; he leadeth me the quiet waters by." The familiar words of this metrical psalm wafted down the hall. They were sung by an obviously untrained voice, sung to my most favorite tune, "Crimond" right from the Scottish Psalter.

But they were not being sung by a Scotsman, but by a Dutchman named John*, from the other branch of the Calvinists.

This was surprising, because not ten minutes ago, John had been cursing out a nurse for putting his water out of reach. He already had a reputation for hating women, evidenced by his angry treatment of his wife. His rigid standards of righteousness, as well as his flagrant violation of them were becoming legendary.

His pastor, from a smaller breakaway sect of the Dutch Reformed Church, visited regularly. I was glad he did, because that meant I didn't have to. Or so I thought.

Joseph P. Smith

The problem was the fact that John had problems taking orders from a woman. This led to constant loud quarrels. Somehow, it seemed to be the chaplain's job to keep him quiet. I'd try to do it by engaging him in theological debate. He could be insistent there; stubborn as a mule, but usually controllable.

He asked me if I was a Calvinist. I told him that I had always thought I was, until the real ones told me differently. He was insistent that an unbeliever couldn't do anything righteous.

"Can he give blood to the Red Cross? "I asked.

"His motives won't be pure," he responded.

"Are your motives ever pure?" I asked.

"Don't argue with me," he said. "We don't believe in common grace at all."

I find it interesting that this theological term has different meanings to different people. My faith group views this as the good things God pours out on all men. "God causes His sun to rise on the evil and the good, and sends rain on the righteous and the unrighteous." John's group uses it to mean God's enablement, given to men, that allows them to do good things. They deny you can have it if you're not a Calvinist.

I really had no purpose to argue with John about theology. But when he was reciting the doctrines of his church, he was civil, even though he disagreed. That helped our mission on the floor. It was nonsense, but it worked.

Then one day, in the middle of a discussion about the Canons of Dort, his voice changed, and in stentorian tones he announced, "The Lord will not hold him guiltless who taketh his name in vain!"

It was almost as though another personality had taken over. I was ready to use the five criteria for determining the difference between Dissociative Identity Disorder and Demon Possession.

At our Chaplain's prayer meeting, I asked what the others thought. One chaplain, more Calvinistic than I said, "No, I've known John all his life. He's imitating the voice of his pastor."

"But why this verse?" I asked.

"John was only eight years old when his father died. They had a very close relationship, and John was heartbroken. In his shock, he went outside the room and cursed God. Now he wonders if it was the unpardonable sin. He wonders if God could ever forgive him!"

That explained a lot. Then I was surprised at how the doctors interacted with John's behavior. One weekend the oncologist covering the floor for all the others was a lovely Philippina lady. She's heard about John and dreaded his misanthropy. But instead of treating her with anger, as he had other women, he invited her to sit by the bed while he gave her a thirty minute recitation of all his sins. She reacted with stunned amazement.

I wondered how much of the behavior was caused by the tumor. His own doctor insisted that none of it was. He was assured by the anatomy of the tumor. He said, "That thing is so loose, if I took off the top of his head, turned him upside down, and shook, the tumor would fall out."

Joseph P. Smith

I was sure that was an exaggeration, but it vividly told me what I needed to know.

After his surgery, the head nurse beeped me in the middle or the night. "John is moaning and making noise that is keeping others awake. Do you think you could quiet him?"

I said I'd try, and started getting into the clothes I'd laid out.

When I got off the elevator, the first thing that greeted me was the sound of John loudly moaning, "I'm in hell! I'm in hell!"

Before going to his room, I needed to get a handle on his physical situation. So I went to the desk and asked for an assessment of John's pain.

"I know you think that brain surgery is painful," the nurse said, "but it's not. There are no nerve ending pain sensors on the brain or its covering, the dura. The only pain he has if from the scalp incision. That's like a nasty scratch. We've given him some Tylenol. Pain isn't his problem."

If physical pain wasn't, spiritual pain was. I went to John and asked if he could tell me his problem. "I don't know whether I'm one of the elect," he said.

"John, you come to that question because you strongly believe in the sovereignty of God. Right?"

"Yes."

"Well, let me ask you this. Can a sovereign God make a promise?"

The debater in John overtook the moaner. He was thinking so hard his emotions receded.

"That's a trick question, isn't it?"

"Well, yes, John. I guess it is. But it's an important, honest question, isn't it?"

"Well, I guess if I said there was anything a sovereign God couldn't do, I'd be silly."

"Oh no, John. Can a sovereign God break a promise?"

"What do you mean?"

"I mean that God's holiness and righteousness underlie his sovereignty. God can't lie." He's given us His word on that."

"So?"

"So He says in the Bible, 'He that hath the Son hath life; and he that hath not the Son of God hath not life. These things have I written unto you that believe on the name of the Son of God; that ye may know that ye have eternal life,...'

"That means that either you have Him or you don't. 'But as many as received Him, to them gave He power to become the sons of God, even to them that believe on his name:' This means that if you believe in Jesus, it's the evidence that you've received Him. And you can know, right now, that you have eternal life."

"But I still don't know if I'm one of the elect."

"No man can call Jesus Lord, except by the Holy Spirit. Anyone who has not the Spirit of God is none of His. It doesn't matter if our faith, as I believe, preceded our being born into the family of God, or as you believe, followed it. Faith is the evidence of regeneration. If there's faith, you belong to God."

"I don't believe that. You can't know you're in grace until you persevere unto the end."

"What would it take, John, to convince you that you're in grace, and bound for heaven?"

"I'd have to live a perfect life."

"Sorry, John. That's not going to happen. 'If we say we have no sin, we deceive ourselves, and the truth is not in us. But if we confess our sins, He is faithful and just to forgive us our sins, and to cleanse us from all unrighteousness.' God doesn't expect perfection, but honesty."

I suppose this attitude is what his pastor called, admiringly, John's humility. But it was what kept the rest of the floor up at night.

John never got it straight. I didn't really expect him to. In a couple of days, he went home, and was no longer the hospital's problem.

> A garden locked is my sister, my bride,
> A rock garden locked, a spring sealed up.
> Song of Solomon 4:12

Chapter 18
The Child Bride

Expressions of affection often take odd forms. The habitual way people tell each other, "I love you," may not convey that message to anyone else. I had a sense that even my derisive nickname, "Toe Tag Chaplain," was used by the staff to express a kind of regard for me. I tried to be "part of the team" and their willingness to joke about my role was evidence that I was accepted.

But one couple, where the man was the cancer patient had a game going where artificial roles dominated their love life.

He was in his late thirties, and she was about twenty-eight, the mother of two young kids. She was poised and confident but he never treated her that way. It wasn't a put-down, but the only way he could tell her he loved her seemed more appropriate for a parent/child relationship than between lovers.

As I observed and reflected on this role play, I began to understand how it had developed. He was ten years older than she was. He had concentrated on his career in his early adulthood, and had risen in an auto dealership to be a very valuable service department supervisor. He was full of "success" stories about how he had been able to diagnose a car's problem after others had given up.

Joseph P. Smith

There's something about car talk that seems manly in our society. He fit the picture of a "man's man" very well. He was ruggedly handsome, looked extremely fit, and could easily have been the heart-throb of many a young girl. He exuded competence and confidence.

He didn't begin to date until he had risen to his job, owned his own home, and had money in the bank. I never learned much about her background, but got to see how he expressed affection by caring for her. I think he would have done anything for her. My initial reaction to their conversations with each other was to bristle at what I thought was colossal ego. But as time went on, I recognized that devotion better described his role, and that he would have had a hard time had he treated her as an adult, in a way more to my liking. She relished her role, and I eventually came to recognize that their role play was their business, and I needed to let it alone.

They were members of a good church that was between pastors. Although they appreciated my visits, they really weren't "high maintenance" people. I got to love them both. I saw him about once a month, during his chemotherapy treatments.

The cancer began to take its toll. It takes an inordinate amount of nutrition to sustain a tumor, and the tumor gets its share first. Appetite is one of the first victims of cancer. He began to lose weight, and there wasn't much to lose but muscle. The robust chest that showed through his pajama tops was rapidly becoming sunken, and hollow. He looked constantly tired. He seemed to struggle with his new role of dependency.

In his "Autobiography of Dying," Archie Hanlan describes how there can be multiple grief processes in the slow descent into death. Grief is about loss, and every separate loss brings its separate grief. My patient lost his robust appearance, then his strength, and then his alert, diagnostic mind.

But when his wife came to visit, he would get out of bed, pull up a chair, fluff up a pillow, and seat her with all the formality of the white tie dressed ushers of a downtown Chicago church I occasionally attended as a student. If he was hooked up to an IV, this was difficult, but he planned how to do it, and never failed.

As pain became less controlled, this was even more difficult. The only way to manage the symptoms was to keep him in the hospital. When his wife wasn't present, he showed signs of depression, but he never allowed himself to show it to her. His optimism was fading, but he was desperate to keep up appearances while she was there.

One day when his wife wasn't there we got into a conversation about his feelings.

"What's the thing that most concerns you?" I asked.

"How will my wife manage without me," he said.

From what I've seen of her, she'll do very well, I thought. But what I said was, "It seems like you're saying that she's going to be alone."

He retreated from that brink. "Well, I have to face the possibility," he said, as if he were less certain.

Wanting to ease his mind, I tried to gently bring up the subject with his wife. We were sitting together in the day room while he was being examined when I said, "You know, I was talking with your husband the other day, and he was concerned about how you were getting along at home without him. Taking care of you is an important part of his life. How are you doing?"

"It's really not a problem. I'm more concerned about him. The kids are fine. We have good insurance, so the bills are being paid."

"Did he always pay the bills, too?"

"He's very organized. That's one of the reasons he rose in the ranks to his job. If I tried to help, he'd lose track because he didn't do it himself. So I let him. But actually, I kind of like taking care of things. Before, things just seemed to slip by. Now I have things to do to look forward to."

I saw a checkbook peeking out of the top of her purse by her feet. "It looks like you're writing the checks," I said with a nod toward it.

"He had kept the register very well. So it wasn't hard. I just studied the checks that were written regularly, and got on to the pattern."

"Is there anything you noticed he was doing that you improved on?"

"Well, only one thing. We had four insurance policies, and he was making quarterly premium payments on them. That costs extra. So I arranged for the payments to come due in the four different quarters, and started making annual payments."

"Don't throw this at him, but would you "forget" and leave the checkbook on the night stand when you go home tonight. If he looks at it he might be comforted."

There was no way to tell if this little ruse worked, but he stopped worrying about her competence. His worries now involved his father. He would visit, and spend the whole time complaining. The day he complained about his son's moans from pangs of pain, I just about lost it. He wanted his son to "be a man" and accept whatever came.

As my patient was telling me this, almost in tears, I said, "I don't want to take over your life, but you need some help. You've got too many things on your plate. Let me take one of them for you, and I mean your father. It will be easier for me to deal with him."

He agreed to it.

I caught the father coming onto the floor the very next afternoon. "Can you come with me for just a minute into this conference room?" I asked.

He followed me in.

"Your son told me yesterday that you complained when he moaned."

"Yes I did. He used to be a man, and now he's acting like a baby!"

"Well, he's been dealing with significant pain for over two years. Chronic pain has a way of wearing you down. Strong men can take severe pain for a little while, but even minor pain which persists a long time can get to you. And remember, he's been weakened by the cancer so he's battling without strength. He deserves a break."

"Well, I taught him to be a man. I don't want to see him sniveling."

Joseph P. Smith

With all the calmness I could muster, I got right into his face, and said, "If you can't behave yourself in front of him, you may get your wish. I don't remember you're being with him that much. So just you pull that stunt again, and I will take you picture and give it to hospital security, and we won't let you in the room again!"

I wondered if he had any idea how empty the threat was. But he did visit and I never heard of his making any more trouble.

The attention turned to his kids. It started when the head nurse called the wife aside, and said, "I know our rules say that children can't visit in the hospital, but they haven't seen him in a while. I'm sure if you want to bring them, I can get the rules relaxed so they can see their dad."

She didn't respond but started thinking, and finally came to me with her dilemma. "I want the kids to remember their dad as he was. He looks bad now, and I wonder how seeing that will shock them."

"My advice would be to give them a blank sheet of paper and some crayons and ask them to draw a picture of what their very sick dad looks like in the hospital. If he really looks better than the picture, bring them."

They came, and the little boy climbed into the bed and laid on his shoulder and chest, while the little girl sang a song she had learned in school. The tears didn't flow from my patient's eyes until they were gone. Two weeks later, he was in the land of no tears.

*"Oh that my words were written!
Oh that they were inscribed in a book!"
Job 19:23*

Chapter 19
The Bible Battle

"Half of our board members are Gideons! How will we ever explain this to them?"

All of our chaplains, from all six hospitals, met once a month at 6:30am for announcements and prayer. The Grand Rapids hospital chaplaincy was not the creation of the hospitals. It was supported by the gifts of about 30 churches and 300 individuals, and was administered by an independent, self-perpetuating board, containing some pastors but mostly Christian businessmen. My predecessor as director had asked to be relieved of the direction of the chaplaincy, but couldn't bear to leave the ministry entirely. In the hospital he served, he was often still thought of as the director, and because he was such a wise leader of men, this was never a problem.

The hospital was also administered by an independent board. One of the board members had become aware of a Modern English paraphrase of the New Testament, a paperback with artful line drawings throughout the text. Although the Gideon's organization provided free Bibles for every nightstand in the hospital, and this paraphrase of the Bible would become an expense, she wanted it to replace the Gideon Bibles. Other members of the board wanted to hear from the chaplains before making a move.

So they had invited John to a meeting that morning to give testimony about the chaplains' thinking.

Now actually, most of us were in favor of modern language translations. But this one gave us several problems.

First of all, a paraphrase is not constrained to being literal. Rather than a word-by-word translation, it gives a thought-by-thought rendering. Since that requires interpretation, the result can be biased by the thinking of the one making the paraphrase. However there was a greater problem.

The publisher's goal was a version that would be understood by young readers. While the intent may have only been simplified language, the linguists also decided that anything that would offend the sensibilities of young reader should be sanitized. The result was to gut the descriptions of the central theme of the New Testament, which was the atoning death of Jesus Christ, because they were too bloody. Therefore this paraphrase was not theologically accurate.

But the otherwise competent hospital board wasn't gifted theologically, so this would seem like an arcane argument. Besides the paperbacks were cute. John had wondered what he could say that would sway the board. We prayed that God would guide him. But even up to the time of the meeting, no such guidance came.

The hospital board members were seated around a boardroom table with the two Bible versions tossed in the center. John was invited into the room,

TALES FROM THE TOE TAG CHAPLAIN

but not seated at the table. He had been ushered to a chair against the wall to wait his turn.

Minutes were read, followed by a financial report. That led to discussion of fiscal policy. The board was considering making an offer to settle a lawsuit from a patient whose smoking had started a fire in his loosely wrapped sterile pad. And as the meeting dragged on, the air in the room became more and more clogged with blue cigarette smoke.

This was before Surgeon General's warnings were printed on every pack. But a ***hospital*** board smoking?!

Then, in the midst of the fog (or should I say smog?) the guidance came in a flash.

"Chaplain, what do you think of the idea of replacing the Bibles?"

John stood. He said, "Let me show you something. I want you Archie* to lay your cigarette on the paperback, and you Phyllis* on the Gideon Bible."

The hospital version of the Gideon Bible had a fire proof cover. The paraphrase had a single-layer paper cover. First it curled. A dark circle formed where the cigarette touched. Within one minute, a little blaze popped up.

The chairman of the board poured water from his drinking glass on it.

"I've seen enough," he said. "Is there any discussion?"

John called me with the news as soon as he left the room. It was a round one TKO for the Gideon Bible.

My Father,
if this cannot pass away unless I drink it,
Your will be done." Matthew 26:42

Chapter 20
Preventing Divorce

"I wish you could find time to look in on Joyce*. She's a member of our church in good standing. But right now, she has a lot on her plate, and can use extra help."

Ordinarily we tried to stay out of the way of the pastor, when a person registered as a member of a local church. But in this case, I was asked by the pastor to look in on a case of one of his people. He was actually one of our board members.

I appreciated that he did not share his understanding of the situation. It indicated that he trusted me, and wanted a fresh evaluation. And the fact was, she did have a lot on her plate.

"Hi, I'm Chaplain Smith, assigned to this floor. Your pastor, Dr. Fxxxxx, has asked me to stop in. He's not abandoning you. But he thinks you need all the help you can get."

"I'm sorry to bother you, but I have a situation that has taken me by surprise. I'm not sure what to do."

"You've just recently been diagnosed with cancer. Is that what is surprising you?"

"Of course that was a shock. But no, I'm talking about a situation with my husband. He's a public official in the government of our suburb. Just a couple of months ago, he confronted me with the news that he wants a divorce. He's already moved out, and I think he's already living with his new lover. I thought he didn't believe in divorce. Our church doesn't. I certainly didn't see this coming. I thought we had a good marriage. We have three grown children. They're devastated, too."

"Do you have a lawyer?" I said. "Don't worry about the cost. It will be billed to your husband."

"Yes. He's already gotten the courts to award me temporary espousal support. But he says that since Michigan is a no-fault state, my husband can file without blaming me. He just needs to say there are irreconcilable differences. The court usually orders marriage counseling. They give that two years to work, and then if he still wants the divorce, he gets it."

"And you want him back?"

"Yes. I still love him. And he's making a terrible mistake. I don't want him to suffer for it."

She seemed sincere. But most women in this situation just lash out. They are so angry, they can't examine their own motives. It would take more than this statement to convince me she was primarily concerned about him.

"Has he talked with Dr. Fxxxx?"

"Pastor invited him to come to the church office, and had me there to listen."

"What did Larry* say?"

He said, "Pastor, you won't believe this, but I believe God has spoken to me, and wants me to divorce my wife and marry my girlfriend."

"And what did the pastor say?"

"He said, 'You're right. I don't believe God told you to violate His Word.'"

"How did your husband respond?"

"He said, 'Well then, we have a difference of opinion.'" She went on, "he's a pretty stubborn man."

I probed, "What worries you most?"

"I'm worried about his soul. This is not just a moment of sin. It's choosing to wallow in it. I'm sure he will be punished."

"Are you both members of the church?"

"Right now we are. But Pastor has warned Larry that if he goes on with this, he will be excommunicated."

"That's not the reason I asked. Your church requires a profession of faith for member-ship. That means Larry has told the deacons that He believes in Jesus for salvation, and has been born again. If what he said was true, your church teaches he is eternally secure, that he's a child of God, and nothing can change that. But you're say you're still worried."

"Well, I am. Larry says he trusts Jesus. But Jesus condemns divorce. So Larry's behavior isn't consistent with faith in Christ. The book of Hebrews in the Bible says that God chastises His children, and that if you can sin and get away with it, it's because you're not really a child of God."

Tales from The Toe Tag Chaplain

She quoted Hebrews 12:5-8.

> My son, do not regard lightly the discipline of the Lord, Nor faint when you are reproved by Him;
> For those whom the Lord loves He disciplines,
> And He scourges every son whom He receives.
>
> It is for discipline that you endure; God deals with you as with sons; for what son is there whom *his* father does not discipline? But if you are without discipline, of which all have become partakers, then you are illegitimate children and not sons.

She had a level of sophistication in her theology that most people in her church didn't share. And it was right on, correct in every detail.

"For you to accomplish what you want, you'll need expertise I don't have. But if what you say is true, it isn't selfish. And that allows us to pray in faith."

So after praying for God to intervene, I went on my way.

The next day, I could see her crying as I passed the door, so I reversed course and asked, "Is there some new problem, dear one."

She responded, "My son is furious. He's dropped out of college and come home. I don't think our problems should affect his education.."

Joseph P. Smith

As if she didn't have enough to worry about, this was also dumped on her.

"Oh, my! We need the hand of God to intervene. Let's pray specifically about this."

Her facial response to my praying showed the conflict she was dealing with. It was hard to leave her, but I had other needy people.

The next day she was discharged, and I didn't see her again for several weeks. But when her name popped up in the intake records, I made a call on her a priority.

"What's going on now?" I asked, wanting to let her talk about more than medical symptoms.

"My prayers have been answered." she glumly replied.

"You don't seem happy," I said.

"Well, I got a bill from the hospital, and the co-pay on my treatment was more than I could afford on my temporary espousal support, So I went to my attorney and told him I needed an increase. He said those were not easy to get, because the court is reluctant to reopen something already decided. He said that I'd need a good reason.

"I said that I had cancer, and that chemotherapy co-pays were very high. His response surprised me. He leaned back in his chair and said, 'You know, you've done it!'"

I said, 'Done what?'

"'Prevented the divorce. As long as you have cancer, the State of Michigan won't let him divorce you.'

Tales from The Toe Tag Chaplain

"Chaplain Smith, that means the only way I can prevent the divorce is to stay sick. If I recover, it sets Larry free to do something stupid. I don't know how I should pray!"

I was stunned. Conflict upon conflict was being inflicted on this woman. I often don't know what to say, but it rarely keeps me from saying something. This was one of those rare times. I just took her hand, as a tear started. She reached for a tissue on the night stand and wiped my face.

"Oh God," I began the prayer, "I don't know what to ask for. This dear woman is so troubled and confused by these impossible circumstances, that all we can do is cry out to you. In your wisdom, show us what to do. Calm our hearts, and meet her concern for Larry* also. How good it is to have an all-wise God so close to us, yet ruling over the stars in their courses, and all the affairs of men. We are forced to trust You! Oh, God, help us to trust you!!"

Her monthly treatments went on for several years. There was no way for her to be happy. But she faced her illness all that time, not only not sure if God would heal her, but not sure she should want to be healed. Her condition slowly worsened. All hope seemed to fade away.

One day she asked me to lean over to listen to her weak voice.

"At least, I'll be gone, and Larry won't be a bigamist."

That was our last contact. I never saw her again. But the newspaper got events in the order she wanted. The obituary appeared before the wedding announcement.

> ...they shall answer and say,
> 'Our hands did not shed this blood,
> nor did our eyes see it.
> Deuteronomy 21:7

Chapter 21
The Bat Boy

The sound of the beeper had become obnoxious. I was getting an average of four hours sleep a night, and abusing coffee to stay awake. But it was the emergency room of my own hospital, calling at about 1:00 am. So I called in right away.

"No hurry, Chaplain. A couple in Fremont was bludgeoned badly. The man was pronounced on the scene, but the woman is being airlifted here, and will be here any minute. But she's barely hanging on. We need you to minister to friends and relatives, but they'll be coming by car, so it'll be about an hour."

I got there in half that time. The woman was still in the ER, and they were working on her frantically. I would have thought they would have her in an OR already, but there wasn't time just yet to find out what was going on.

I had a chance to question the helicopter's EMTs.

"Do you know who's coming?"

There's a teenage son and daughter who are coming with their married sister and her husband. There will surely be others. The boy came home from a basketball game and found them.

Tales from The Toe Tag Chaplain

I turned to the ER Desk. "We'd better get a room ready for them away from the ER waiting room. It will be hard to comfort them if we don't have any privacy."

"I think we can use the conference room. There're chairs for about twenty, and of course, a big table."

She showed me a large conference room, two doors down the hall from the interior entrance to the ER. In the hall outside, was a food service cart, empty of everything but a suggestion.

"Could we get some coffee, maybe some cookies and a portable coat rack in here? Then you'll be able to direct visitors to us, and keep the waiting room clear of them. I'll offer to get updates from you about every hour, and keep the family's questions from getting in the way."

I got my overcoat hung up, and was getting a cup of coffee with dry cream (I call it plaster dust) when four people came in. The teen girl was crying softly, the older couple seemed composed, but the boy got my attention right away. His eyes were locked in a vacant stare. He didn't move to take off his coat, or get to a chair. He just stood in the room, obviously in shock.

I went to him, put my arm around his shoulder and said, "We're going to do everything that can be done for you mother. She's in very good hands. This is a Level I Trauma Center; we have everything to use that is available anywhere. I'm Chaplain Smith, and I'm going to be updating you on her condition frequently. It could be a while before we know what her chances are. She's taken an awful beating, but the good news is that she's still alive, and she's here, where she'll get world class help.

"It'll be a little while before I check up on progress, so let me take your coat, and then we'll get you seated and bring a drink for you. Would you like some coffee here, or should I get you some pop?"

He didn't respond. His coat was unbuttoned, so I helped him take it off and showed him to a seat. He hadn't responded to my offer of a drink, but I poured a Styrofoam cup of black coffee, set it in front of him, and reached for the sugar and creamer boxes. A swizzle stick completed the supply. Pausing, I repeated my offer to get a can of pop. He still hadn't responded, so I turned to the older couple and said, "What else can I do to help?"

"We're OK Chaplain," the sister's husband said. "John* was at a high school basketball game, and must have go before we brought Nancy* home from where she had been babysitting. After we dropped her off, we waited to check if she got in ok, because it was below zero. In just a minute she came running back out, screaming. My wife held her while I ran into the trailer. My father-in-law was laying over the coffee table in the living room, his head a bloody mess."

The wife continued the story, "When I got in with Nancy, we saw that the light was on in the front bedroom. There was a bloody ball bat in the doorway. Inside we found my mother on the bed and Johnny curled up on the floor, in shock. My husband called 911 right away and the sheriff's deputies called for the helicopter. The deputies put yellow tape around the crime scene, and the medics checked mom and dad. They couldn't get any response from dad, but they loaded mom in the helicopter and told us to come here."

"Do you need a telephone to call other next-of-kin? I think we can plug one in here. Don't worry about charges. We just want to help."

They began calling and people began arriving. After each visit to the ER to get updates, I prayed. They happily gave permission. The rest of the time I sat by the boy, who still hadn't spoken a word.

At about 5:00am, three deputy's from Newaygo County came in, headed straight for John, and announced, "John Xxxxxx, you are under arrest for the murder of Xxxxx Xxxxx and the attempted murder of Yyyyy Xxxxxx. Anything you say can and will be used against you in a court of law. You have a right to remain silent. You have a right to an attorney. If you cannot afford an attorney one will be provided for you. Do you understand your rights?"

He still didn't speak. As I followed them out the doctor told me, "Mrs. Xxxxx passed away about five minutes ago.

I gave the standard "we gave it our best" speech to all those in the conference room, all the while thinking, *I just spent three hours comforting a murderer.*

There's no way to knoiw what a day will be like, or a night in this case. There also was no way after all this to get back to sleep.

Therefore God gave them over
in the lusts of their hearts to impurity,
so that their bodies
would be dishonored among them.
Romans 1:24

Chapter 22
Come Out!
Come Out,
Wherever You Are!

I never saw it coming.

He wasn't even my patient. He'd probably spent many days in our department, and I would have never met him, except I recognized his father. A chance meeting in the hallway was how I knew this well-known deacon in a local church had a son with cancer. The boy was a fifteen-year-old, scrubbed clean example of conservative evangelical Christianity. And when I got to know him, his cancer was very advanced.

I was impressed with the depth of the relationship he had with his father. They always prayed together when they met. The father seemed to "tune in" on his son's concerns. They were equally comfortable talking about spiritual things and Sparky Anderson, the Detroit Tiger manager. The boy called him "Captain Hook" because of how quick he was to call on the bull pen when a pitcher faltered. I promised the boy's dad that I'd look in on him.

The news from the doctors wasn't good. Several treatment plans had been tried, but his tumors were still growing.

Our doctors tended to avoid emotionally loaded words. We never named a case as terminal. Rather, the test results were read in detail, assessed as to whether they were good news or bad, and they left it with that. But after weeks of negative reports, all of us were worried.

"Tell me how I'm doing," he said on one of my visits.

"I leave the medical issues to the medical people," I said. "But you're probably aware that things don't look good."

"Am I going to die?"

"We're all going to die," I said. "What you want to know is, will it be soon. I think you should ask the doctor that, point blank, if you really want to know. It looks to me like they haven't given up, so maybe there are more things to try."

"I need to know."

"People usually say, 'I want to know, or I don't want to know.' But you didn't phrase it that way. Seems like there's more to the story."

He looked away. I could hear the clock ticking. We were obviously waiting for him to decide whether to confide something to me. I tend to think that usually, it doesn't help for me to talk. So I just sat there while he struggled.

Joseph P. Smith

As he started to talk, he looked at me, but then turned away and said, "I'm a homosexual."

As I say, I didn't see it coming. I almost thought I hadn't heard correctly, but then quickly realized that was denial on my part. I'd heard correctly alright.

"What makes you say that?" I wasn't sure what direction to take the conversation. I was still reeling.

"I do homosexual things. And I enjoy it. I look forward to another opportunity. I have no interest in girls."

"There are lots of fifteen-year-olds who have no interest in girls. When did this start."

"I was twelve. A bunch of us were having a slumber party, and I was sharing a blanket on the floor with an older boy. He asked me if I wanted to watch, and then he did some things that seemed interesting.

"As he told me some of the details, my heart sank. It seemed like an inadvertent teen experiment, nut with disastrous results. got himself off.

He ended by saying, "That's how it started."

"My guess is that your parents don't know, right?"

"Oh, man, I hope they never find out!"

"Well, don't worry, I'm not going to tell them. But you need a safe place to talk about this and sort out your feelings. I understand how you feel at odds with your parents. But there's a lot to this stuff, and more that we don't know than what we do know. But first thing is, you may be jumping to a conclusion. Lots of people who have done homosexual things, don't turn out to be homosexuals. In fact, I'm a little bothered about calling anyone a homosexual. That makes behavior into an identity."

"But I want to do it. And I didn't choose to want it. It's a real piece of trouble. It must be that's who I am."

"Maybe you're right. And then, maybe not. I'm not satisfied that the research into this isn't biased. I have a lot of trouble with present day thinking about this. So just let me tell you what I think we know for sure, and what we shouldn't be so sure about.

"People argue about what causes this. In all those arguments I've heard about, they try to blame it on one cause. We just don't know if it could be caused by hundreds of different things. Just because we can't find one cause that fits all cases, doesn't mean there aren't causes. You say, and so do others, that you didn't choose to be a homosexual, and I believe you. Others did choose it. I know women who have reacted to abuse by men. Whether that was the cause of their orientation, or just a historical event that uncovered it, is beyond me.

"Sex is a gift from God. If it wasn't so nice, there might not be a human race. Sexual experience is powerful. People have done crazy things for sex. I had a woman parishoner once whose dad had used her sexually from the time she was ten until she went away to college. She felt soiled by it, really rotten. But when she was away from home, she felt she couldn't go on without it."

"Sexual pleasure is so wonderful that even when someone abuses us, our bodies can betray us, and enjoy it. When we find a way to make that pleasure always happen, it makes us lock in on that way. It's called a fetish.

"I know people who did homosexual things as adolescents. As adults, they're not interested in the slightest. But when it becomes the regular way they get sexual release, people often get stuck in it.

"All, or at least most boys go through a stage when they're not interested in girls. But that usually isn't sexual. I can't prove anything about this, but I wonder that if the boy becomes sexualized before he begins to be interested in girls, if he doesn't get stuck there.

"But what I know for sure, is that the Bible does not condemn us for feelings we don't seek. We can toy with our affections, and God may even be judgmental about that, but what He clearly condemns is a homosexual act. No matter what your feelings are, doing homosexual things is something we are not supposed to do.

"There's a matter of choice here. A person may be severely tempted to do these things, but he's responsible not to do them."

"But it just happened. God must have made me this way!"

"There's no way you could ever prove that. People claim they can prove it because they were always that way. They say that proves it's the way God made them. But the Bible says that's not the way God made us. We have these urges to do wrong things because of our fallen nature. All of us deal with that. I'm not in the least tempted to do sex with another male, but I am tempted to use my sexual nature outside of the way God intended. I'm Ok there. But it's always a struggle. Not every fallen nature has the same twist to it, but we're all twisted."

"That's why I'm worried. Will I go to hell?"

"That's where we all should go. But God forgives sin. This is sin, but to Him, it's no harder to forgive than any other sin. We all sin and all need forgiveness. Have you ever asked Jesus to be your Savior? Do you trust Him?"

"When I was about five, I became a Christian. I asked Jesus to save me."

"Did you come to trust Him?"

"Yes. I trusted him to save me."

"But did you trust Him for anything else?"

"What do you mean?"

"The Bible says, 'For God so loved the world that He gave His one and only Son, that whoever believes in Him, should not die, but have everlasting life.' That doesn't just mean to believe there is a God, or even just to believe Jesus died for us. The Bible never puts limits on that faith.

"For instance, in John chapter eight, it says that some Jews believed on him. But He said, 'If you continue in My word, *then* you are truly disciples of Mine; and you will know the truth, and the truth will make you free.'

"They declared that they were the offspring of Abraham, and had always been free. Now that wasn't true. They had nationally been slaves in Egypt, under Babylonian captivity, and at that moment, any Roman soldier could have ordered them to stop what they were doing and carry his bags up to a mile.

"The upshot of it all was that though they believed Jesus about some things, they were stuck on the idea that they had special privileges with God. They wanted to pick and choose about whether any particular thing Jesus said was true. That means they agreed on some things, but not others. They really didn't put their trust in Jesus. They only believed what He said when it fit in with what they had 'always' believed.

"So, when you trusted Christ, did you have any reservations?"

"No. I was a little child."

"Then the Bible says, 'But as many as received Him, to them He gave the right to become children of God, *even* to those who believe in His name.' If you've trusted Him fully, you're a child of God, and that can never be changed. But do you now believe that the Bible says that these acts are sin?"

"My friend says his pastor believes the Bible doesn't really teach that."

"That's a pretty risky thing to say. It's pretty clear that pastor doesn't take the Bible seriously. But if you are a child of God, and if this is sin, you will be disciplined for it. But you can't lose your place in heaven."

"Just don't tell my folks."

"You can count on that. It's one of the things that's really good about hospital chaplaincy. We make a safe place to wrestle with your inmost thoughts."

"Thanks."

- -

Tales from The Toe Tag Chaplain

That wasn't the end of it. We had many other sessions together. In the end, he wasn't convinced he could ever be attracted to a girl, but the constraints of the hospital had proved to him that he could be celibate.

And he was just the first of six who came out to me over the years I was flattered that I looked like a safe place to them. All of them had different stories. All of them came to the same conclusion. And all of them died. Only one did not remain celibate.

> ...the younger son gathered everything together and went on a journey into a distant country... Luke 13:15

Chapter 23
The Runaway Son

"Hi. I'm Chaplain Smith. You're a new patient on this floor, and I always check in to see if there's any way I can help. Your intake records don't show a church. Is that right?"

"Well, there is a church, but we haven't been there a long time. We don't even know the present pastor, or even if there is one."

"Then, would you like for me to pray for you, or read some Scripture?"

The couple looked at each other. I thought they wondered who should answer. Finally, the woman in the chair said, "I don't know what good it could do. We've done a lot of praying."

"That sounds like you have some real concerns. I don't have miracles in my back pocket, but if you're troubled, I do care. Is it something you can share?"

Again there was a pause. This time I was sure she was hoping the man in the bed would speak, but was ready if he didn't.

"You see, Reverend, we never could have any children. So when I was forty-one, we decided to adopt. He was a wonderful baby boy, and we loved him. He grew up very bright, even won a scholarship to college that made it easier for us.

"He was an Eagle Scout, earned the God and Country badge that was awarded in front of our whole church. And went off to Yale, seeming to be headed for a great life. But he got in with some VietNam war protesters, and became obsessed with it.

"As far as we know, he never burned his draft card, and he was never drafted. But one day he just left school and disappeared, we don't know where. He left everything in his dorm room. All that was gone was about half of his underwear, some tee shirts and walking shorts, and his gym bag. We tried to forward letters, to no avail. That was before we had email. More than twenty years went by. We finally concluded that since he was such a good boy, he must have a good reason for leaving it all behind. And since neither of us can believe he's in any trouble, we decided we'd just wait until he was ready to get back in touch."

"But now you want to find him? What changed?"

"His father was assigned to Hospice care this morning. We don't have long until we can't both see him again. It feels strange to try to hunt him down, because we trust him, and it feels like betrayal. But we don't have much time."

"Are you wondering how he will feel if you find him when he doesn't want to be found."

"Yes. Dad wants to say good bye. We both want to know he's all right."

"Ok. I have a suggestion. Suppose you write a letter, explaining the situation, and hire a detective

Joseph P. Smith

to locate him, and have the detective give him the letter. You could instruct the detective not to tell you where he is, and leave the response up to your boy."

"Where can you find such a detective," they asked together.

"Well, I don't know how you can be sure of how good he is, but I've seen an ad in the yellow pages for the "Fat Man" detective agency. The ad says one of their services is to find missing persons. I have no way of checking up on the quality of their work, but if you want to risk a sum of money, it might be worth it. There's a phone book in the night stand."

"We'll talk it over, the wife said.

"In the meantime, suppose I pray for God's direction and a successful search."

It was a little presumptuous, because they hadn't yet decided to call, but their agreement with the offer said I could be sure they'd do it.

"Dear Father. Here's a dear couple who poured their lives into an adopted son, and never asked anything in return. But they love their boy, and want to be sure he's ok and that his leaving doesn't mean he doesn't love them. What we need today is guidance for them to find the right way to search for him, and the right way to approach him, so he doesn't resent their searching. We have no right to ask this, but we believe Jesus' description of you as a loving Father. You must understand their feelings. Help them to feel your loving arms surrounding them. The desire of their hearts is a noble desire. Oh, God, please grant their every request, both those spoken and those too difficult to say. Oh, Shepherd of all lost sheep, grant this humble request in Jesus' name. Amen."

We shook hands in tears, and I went down the hall.

One of the hardest things to do as a chaplain is to not take the ministry of one room into the next. The next people you see have their own drama. And it's the same way when you go home. Your eight-year-old's broken kite isn't the biggest tragedy you've seen that day, but it's his <u>only</u> tragedy. I needed to be totally in whatever setting I found myself, totally committed to that story.

There are two guiding concepts in my chaplaincy. One is that I will always focus on the patient's agenda, and the second is that I will always remember that my life's aim as a Christian minister is to rightly relate people to God. But to do that, I need to find my agenda somewhere in theirs.

The next time I saw these folks, they were busy, with pads full of notes, and the telephone handy. "How's it going?" I said.

"Well," she said, "The detective has our letter, and has given us a list of things that can help him find our son. We're trying to get them together. Some were easy. We had his Social Security number on a card in my wallet. His dorm address at college was easy too. But he wants credit card numbers, and employer's addresses for summer jobs, and a lot of other stuff. I don't know where to find half the stuff, but it feels good to be doing something. I just hope Dad can get the rest he needs."

"Do you mind if I let the other staff know what is going on? It might be better if we did this frantic stuff somewhere else, so Dad can rest."

Joseph P. Smith

"No! I want to be in on this. If you went to another room, I'd just be worried," he said.

"Ok. But with your permission, I'm going to ask if there's something that can relieve some of your anxiety without taking you out of it all. Remember, you're a pretty sick puppy."

After we got the Xanax in him, I offered to read Scripture. I believe the Bible is like a pharmacy, with many good medicines on it's shelves. But you don't blindly reach for some bottle, any bottle and use it on any patient. I try to match the passage to the felt needs of the listeners. I can't think of a better fit than this one.

"What man among you, if he has a hundred sheep and has lost one of them, does not leave the ninety-nine in the open pasture and go after the one which is lost until he finds it? When he has found it, he lays it on his shoulders, rejoicing. And when he comes home, he calls together his friends and his neighbors, saying to them, 'Rejoice with me, for I have found my sheep which was lost!'"

I said, "That's the heart of the Father. You can be sure he understands exactly how you feel. Please, trust His heart."

But the next morning the news was bad. Dad had entered into a coma. I was in the room, kneeling by the bed, holding his hand when he passed into eternity.

His wife went to the phone and called the detective office. "It's too late, call off the search," was all she said.

Tales from The Toe Tag Chaplain

    I never found a place for my agenda, and I'm not sure of anybody's relationship with God. But I still had to go home and play with a kite.

I can count all my bones.
They look, they stare at me;
Psalm 22:17

Chapter 24
American Gothic

"We have an unusual situation here. Because of denominational rivalry, churches here were being burned. So the government, to stop this, made all the church buildings government property. I have to be careful about holding Bible classes in homes. The government may decide that it's really a church and confiscate it!"

It was an eye opening letter from a classmate, now a foreign missionary. He was planting churches, something that I have also done. But the context of his work was so different than mine, that it forced me to think outside the box.

One of the things I've noticed about ministry is that often times, the training isn't very practical. Aspiring doctors may begin to see patients in their second year of pre-medical school. Pastors don't see parishioners until they graduate and receive their first call. They start personal interviews with people without a plan. In fact, they're usually pretty nervous about it. So if they come up with a formula that seems to work, they embrace it like it was a survival strategy. This may lock them into a lifetime of artificial behavior, never reflecting on it.

My lifeline was my correspondence with so many classmates who were in different settings.

Tales from The Toe Tag Chaplain

Their context demanded ministry examination. Keeping in touch with them expanded my world, and freed me from the limitation of a narrow ministry. In the context of the hospital, it frequently became the basis of otherwise unlikely relationships.

I ran into a classmate in the halls of the hospital who was a missionary to the Congo. He was with the pastor of a local church, not a sister church of my own, but close enough to us that we supported some of the same missionaries, all working in interdenominational ministry.

Of course, we greeted one another gladly, as we hadn't seen each other since graduation. In courtesy, he introduced me to the pastor saying that he was going to visit a boy from a family my missionary friend had once stayed with, while on "home assignment" reporting to this sending church.

The pastor inquired whether I had visited the boy. I had not, because he had evident pastoral care. But the pastor invited me to the room to introduce me to the sixteen year old. They told me he had a rare form of lymphoma, the only case we ever had in our hospital.

I began making short, friendly visits, not actually pastoral care, but just friendly chats. One day when I was in the room, his doctor came in. I excused myself. But the doctor sought me out later.

"Do you know this kid?" he asked.

"Not really, He's the parishioner of a church in which a college classmate of mine is a supported missionary. My classmate introduced me to the pastor, and the pastor introduced me to the patient. That's complicated, I know, but you didn't seek me out to just chat. Why is my knowing this kid an issue."

"Well, as you know, the origin of most cancers is the result of an unfortunate collision between a hereditary flaw and an environmental carcinogen. But this cancer is so rare, we wonder if we've got it right. If we've correctly diagnosed this, it's caused by a virus, and the only place where that virus is found is in the African Congo River area. It doesn't make sense."

"Well, it might. Could that virus be carried by someone who doesn't get cancer?"

"Why do you ask?"

"My classmate is a missionary to the Congo River area. He has stayed in this kid's home for a couple of weeks."

"I don't know...."

The doctor's brow wrinkled as he drifted off in thought. He didn't need me anymore, and I went back to my rounds.

It all made me think of how much reading doctors have to do to keep current, and how important it was for them to document their cases so that others could benefit from reading their notes.

It became a back and forth exercise for them, reading all they could and taking tests to confirm that what they were looking at was congruent with what they were reading. All this took place away from the boy, but his case became the intellectual property of everyone there.

Often as I dropped in, his mother and grandmother were there. I got the impression that their main goal was to do the thing Christians would approve. They sat likes birds on a telephone wire, arms folded, faces as blank as those in Grant Wood's famous painting. The whole scene reminded me of a wake, as if the boy were already dead.

They were disdainful of me, probably, I felt, because I didn't fill the role of a chaplain. While they were there I often didn't read scripture or pray formally. But then, I in fact, disdained their faithfulness, because I didn't see any personal warmth.

When they weren't there, I often prayed aloud. I didn't have scripture readings as such, but we often talked about scriptures he had found helpful. His symptoms were well controlled, and the need that was most evident was that he was bored. So one day I taught him to play "battleships," using yellow legal pads from the charting area, and drawing the grid with soft lead pencils.

That seemed to help. But it took an inordinate amount of my time. I was glad there was no supervisor looking at me play games, and was conflicted about what I was not doing while engaged in this frivolity. But who could he play with? Other teens didn't visit. So I began to wonder if I could turn the daily wake with his relatives into game time.

One day they were out in the hall waiting for a doctor's visit to end. Knowing that turning their visits into something less formal was a long shot, I began with a compliment.

"I want to commend you two for your faithful visits. You're here almost every day, and you stay for hours."

"Thank you."

Joseph P. Smith

"One thing I've noticed is that there are no friends who visit."

"Well the truth is he doesn't have many friends. There's no one he's close to."

"Why is that? He's such a nice guy. He should be able to make friends easily."

"People his age aren't interested in spiritual things. He doesn't have much in common with them."

"What does he do for fun?

After a short pause he mother said, "I really don't know. I've never thought about it."

"Isn't he interested in fun times?"

"Well, we go to church together, three times a week."

"What's the most interesting thing to him about church?"

"Hearing missionary reports. He's always interested in new things."

"Yes. He's bored. There's not much to stimulate him here."

"I don't know what we can do about that. We do bring him magazines from different mission boards. I know he reads them."

"He's a pretty quick reader. He's got a lot of time on his hands. And it would be rude of him to be reading while you came to visit. We need something for you to do with him while you're visiting.

Just the other day, I got him to play "battleships" with me. He seemed to like that."

Tales from The Toe Tag Chaplain

"What's that?"

I explained the game to them. "It's easy to do, why don't you try it?"

"I don't think we would remember all the rules."

"Let him teach you. You all have lots of time. I'm on duty here, and I shouldn't take time."

"We could try it. It doesn't seem to have anything sinful about it."

That answer gave me a jolt. This was before the time of "Grand Theft Auto." My mind didn't usually select games based on the warning, "Watch out! It might be sinful."

She went on, "No, we don't have any in the house. They cost so much."

"Well, try this one. It's free!"

I was pleased that later on I often saw them poring over the grids on their legal pads, calling out their shots.

The treatments became drastic. While chemo was being administered by IV, a nurse sat by watching his vital signs, with a syringe full of a "rescue shot" in case the toxic chemicals started to shut down his whole system. It seemed like a game of "chicken," where you scored by how close to death you could go. If I hadn't had explicit faith in our doctors, I would have been troubled no end.

Then, one day, he just wasn't there. I didn't want to know what happened. I never saw an obituary in the paper, so I assumed he was ok.

> "O you who sit in the gardens,
> My companions are listening
> for your voice—
> Let me hear it!"
> Song of Solomon 8:13

Chapter 25
A Genteel Lady

I come to the garden alone, while the dew is still on the roses...

My mother's favorite song wafted out of the room and warmed the hall. I had no idea of its origin, but I wanted to see the source of the music. Propped up in the bed was a very pretty lady, probably about sixty years old, dressed in a lace trimmed nightgown that came up to her chin.

"Hi. I'm Chaplain Smith. You're not on my call list, but the song is one my mother used to sing when she thought she was alone. It was her favorite. I just had to see who was singing."

"Yes. I learned it in the hymn book when I was growing up. But our newer denominational hymn book doesn't have it. It's too sentimental, they say. But I just can't help being sentimental about my Savior. Another one I like is 'He Is So Precious to Me.' I suppose that's too sentimental also."

I replied, "You seem more like my Mom all the time. She is Irish most of the time. That means she is from Ulster, the part of the Irish island that is still in the United Kingdom. Most people think every protestant there is either in the Anglican or Presbyterian Church, but she was Methodist. She learned those songs in the Old Country, growing up."

"Well, that explains it! I'm Stella*, the wife of the Methodist pastor of two small churches south of here. So you're a Methodist?"

"No. During the depression my folks moved out to the country area as a survival strategy. Then when World War II happened with its gas rationing, we couldn't get to the church of their choice, which was Wesleyan, but not Methodist. I grew up attending a little country church that was in a very liberal denomination. I went through their catechism, was even the star of the class, but I wasn't really a believer. They usually had confirmation Sunday on Palm Sunday, but because of me, they had to push it back to Easter."

"How was that?"

"My father was raised in a Methodist Church in the mountains of West Virginia, but as a teenager, joined the Salvation Army. Mother came here when the Salvation Army arranged passage to the United States for women who would become domestic servants. But after a year of that, she quit her job, and joined the Salvation Army, too. Dad played trombone in the New York Salvation Army band, and mom the tambourine. But they never met until they were posted to the same place in Hartford, Connecticut. They had to leave the Salvation Army in the year I was born, because there was no money to pay them. But since the Salvation Army doesn't consider itself a church, I was never baptized. The little country church only found that out just before confirmation Sunday, so they pushed it back one

Joseph P. Smith

Sunday so I could be baptized one week and confirmed the next."

"But you say you weren't a believer. Didn't they ever ask you if you were?"

"Well, they stood all six of us from the catechism class up and asked us to recite the answers to three questions that were printed in the bulletin. I'm not sure any of us really trusted the Lord. I just went through the motions. I was baptized, catechized and fossilized."

"That's so sad."

"I didn't know anything different. I loved the music. Even in the army, when I had an 'A' for atheist on my dog tags, I tried to become a Chaplain's Assistant. I didn't know anyone ever had a personal relationship with God until after I got out of the Army, and was working in an engineering drawing room. I didn't become a believer in church, but through the witness of an engineer at work."

"I understand. We're part of a movement called the 'Good News Movement' in the Methodist Church that emphasizes having a personal relationship with God."

A voice came from behind me. "Well, it seems we have a lot in common." As I turned he went on, "I'm Bill*, Stella's husband."

This was how a warm friendship began. We never discussed our theological differences. Bill was a warm counselor, always ready to listen. He explained that the District Superintendents of the church thought he spent too much time in the town's coffee shops, and not enough in the church office. They wouldn't trust him with a larger city church.

TALES FROM THE TOE TAG CHAPLAIN

But he wanted to be with people, and had the quality of one who listened more than he advised. He loved his work, and was happy in small town settings. I looked forward to seeing them monthly when Stella came in for her chemotherapy. We got on a first name basis.

We always prayed together. Their prayers were warm, not formal. God was a friend to them, one who was like a member of the family. I never sensed any lack of understanding on their part of the transcendence of God. Their informality was not casual. But Jesus was real to them, and they included Him in all parts of their lives. We prayed for each other's children, for our ministries, and for missionaries. Their prayers subjects were always people, real people. The one thing they never brought up for prayer was Stella's illness!

Our relationship became so warm that I confess I began to skip some of the formal protocol that I observed with patients. Even when doors were wide open, I usually knock and make sure patients are ready to see me.

But one day I just walked in without knocking. Stella quickly pulled the sheet up over her face and said, "Oh Joe, I don't want you to see me like this!"

There couldn't have been anything immodest. She was completely hidden. So I said, "I'll leave the room, if you want me to. I'm sorry I didn't knock."

"No," she said, "Don't leave. I just didn't want anybody to see me crying."

As she lowered the sheet to her chin, I saw a swollen face; tear stained cheeks and red ringed eyes.

Joseph P. Smith

"Have you had some bad news?" I asked.

"No. I was having some difficulty swallowing food, and the doctor ordered an endoscope. The anesthetist was pretty rough on me, and I got to feeling sorry for myself. I'm so tired of being sick."

"You never looked very sick when I came to see you. How are things going?"

"We've never talked about it, but I was diagnosed with malignant melanoma almost twenty years ago. That's how long I've had chemo. I come into the hospital once a month to get sick! I'm tired of it."

One of the things I've learned in this ministry is that even minor discomfort, when it is long term, can be psychologically debilitating. There's something about it that just wears you down. I hadn't known she had been treated for twenty years. And she had always before seemed so cheerful.

Her voice became softer as she said to me, "I want to ask you something. Please don't tell Bill. I'm so tired of this treatment. Tell me. If I were to say, 'no more,' would I be committing suicide?"

Answers to questions like this reside in someone who is above my pay grade. She needed my help, but I really didn't know how to answer.

"I don't have a right to answer that question, because I've never suffered like you have. This is between you and your God. But be careful. Most of the time, you don't feel like this. This treatment has enabled you to see your kids grow up, and make you a grandmother. I have many patients who are trying to look ahead, and can't see a future as good as that.

Tales from The Toe Tag Chaplain

But if you make this decision, I won't judge you. I'll be there for you."

We prayed, and I left. I don't know why I didn't want to see Bill this time.

The next day I realized she was still in the hospital. She was out of bed, sitting in a soft chair, dressed in modest pajamas and a beautiful gown.

"I'm surprised you're still here," I said, "What's going on."

"My doctor came in right after you left yesterday. He's usually very brief with me, but yesterday he sat down and seemed a little tentative.

He said, 'You know, all the oncologists in Grand Rapids participate in what is called the Grand Rapids Clinical Oncology program. Each of us takes a particular interest in one kind of cancer. We keep up with the latest published findings about that disease, and maintain a chapter in an ever changing book about that disease. I'm the one who follows Malignant Melanoma. And what I wrote more than twenty years ago, and I've never changed, is that when this skin cancer penetrates below the fat layer under the skin, the patient will be on chemotherapy for the rest of her life. But for the last six months, our scans haven't shown any detectible cancer. That doesn't mean there isn't any; it just means the tumors are too small to see. But I can't help wondering if I'm not treating a cancer that's already gone. So I'm thinking, maybe in this case what I wrote twenty years ago is wrong. I want to continue to follow you with the same scans we've been using, every month for now, and maybe after a while every three months, then six months, and finally yearly. We've got to be sure there aren't tumors too small to see that can start growing again. But are you willing to let us stop the chemotherapy for now?'"

I was stunned. I have seen prayers answered where the beginning of the answer unknown to me came before the prayer. This was an answer to a prayer never prayed.

We rejoiced together. Later Bill came to pick her up in his car. I carried her suitcase beside her wheelchair (hospital protocol), opened the door of the car, and blew them both a kiss as they drove away. I never saw them again.

...sell all that thou hast,
and distribute unto the poor,
and thou shalt have treasure in heaven.
Matthew 18:22

Chapter 26
A Houseful of Antiques

"I'm afraid my children will fight over them."

Chaplains are supposed to deal with spiritual problems. But there's a strange fact that keeps you constantly changing your understanding of what is spiritual. That fact is, that almost everything has a spiritual component to it.

The patient I was talking with was the wife of a psychiatrist, who lived in the same charter township, outside Grand Rapids, where I lived.

Township government was about the only thing our domiciles shared. Many of the highly in demand professionals lived in our township. I lived in the part zoned for single family dwellings, most on fairly small lots. Across the street from me was a housing development platted to take advantage of a government subsidized plan for home ownership. Because of our closeness to that plat, we had natural gas; sanitary and storm sewers; and underground electricity. The plat had a private water supply that allowed the lots to have ten feet less frontage. Not being in the plat, I had my own well for water.

In contrast, she lived in an area zoned for single family farms; where the minimum lot size was sever acres. Of course, there were no working farms there. The farm aspect of the zoning was a fiction to allow acreage for leisure pursuits. A few of the people had a horse or two, only for recreation. But the main function of these types of zones was to allow people who dealt with high stress professions, a bucolic place to hide from the pressure.

Most of the roads had been declared "Natural Beauty" roads. Trees limbs formed a canopy over the dirt road. The classification forbid any modernization, and with it, any travel convenience. Residents wanted privacy and were willing to be inconvenienced for it. One plat in this zone had a plat covenant that didn't allow street signs of house numbers. The township fire department approached them and said, "If you call for a fire truck, how can we find you."

The answer was, "Drive up near here and look for smoke."

Trying to understand the area, my wife and I took the job one winter of delivering the phone books. Houses in this area had between eight and fourteen phones. Everything reeked of money.

My patient's problem was evidence that money doesn't solve everything.

"All my life, I've had a blank check to work with, decorating and furnishing our home. All the furniture is antique cherry wood. The living room has a concert grand piano, made out of cherry, and one hundred twenty years old. I believe it's the only one in the world, and impossible to appraise. There's never been another one on the market, and until this one is auctioned off, we have no idea of what it will bring.

Now that I have cancer, my husband is determined that we need to move into a condominium where there isn't so much to care for. That means not only getting rid of the house and outbuildings, but all the antique furniture that won't go into the condo. All of our family, except maybe my husband, has a lot of sentiment connected with that furniture. I don't think the kids will want me to sell it. And I don't know how to divide it among them without starting a war over it."

If you want to expand the Chaplain's job description to cover this, you've got to have a big expander, I thought. *I sure didn't wake up this morning expecting something like this.*

But I started by exploring who could take the problem. "What does your husband think about it?"

"He says he doesn't want to bother with it. When I tell him it could set our children against each other, he just says, 'Tell them to grow up.'"

So much for the practice of psychiatry! I thought.

"Ok. I don't want to tell you what to do, but I can suggest several ideas. If we can start your thinking, and see that there are ideas that might work, would that ease your mind?"

"Yes, it would."

Joseph P. Smith

"Then, let's start with some basic questions. First of all, would it make any difference to you, about who had what?"

"What do you mean?"

"Well, in our family we had to decide who would get my grandfather's handmade carpenter tools. They were used to do all the fancy interior woodwork in the Greenbrier Hotel, in White Sulphur Springs, West Virginia. That's a five star hotel where everybody from Washington, D. C. Used to spend weekends.

The tools were all stamped with my initials, because I have my grandfather's name, but we decided to have my brother-in-law, in Pulaski, Pennsylvania keep them, because he has a permanent shop where they can be displayed, while I as a minister moved a lot.

What I mean is, do you want there to be a place for some pieces where all of you can see them, and is there such a place?"

"I see, while that would make one of the kids the owner of those pieces, there would be the understanding that they are caretakers, and shouldn't get rid of them."

"Yes. That's the idea. You don't have to think this through now, but it's one of the things you should consider.

"All the kids slept in a very ornate baby bed, a marvel of cabinet making. All of them are already done having babies, but that piece might be one held by someone in trust for all of them."

"Then you might consider that some pieces just fit some of the kids. Are there kids who play the piano? The piano might better be with someone who will play it or has a reason to maintain it."

"I see that. But both girls play."

"You don't have to settle this now, and remember their input is important. Beyond the issues, maybe you should have the pieces without sentimental value appraised, and have them negotiate to divide the furniture so that each one gets equal value. Or maybe just sell them and have the money for them in your estate."

"I see. Those are good ideas. I'll think some more, and at some point I'll get input from them."

"I hope that puts your mind at ease. But now, let's not think about the kids any more today. It's time to think about you. You're facing a very tough, life threatening battle. I want to sort of list the resources you have, so you can use all the tools available to you in that fight. Do you have close family?"

"Just my husband and I at home now."

"Any siblings?"

"No. I'm the last of the Mohicans. I had three siblings, but I'm the only one left."

"How near are your children?"

"The nearest one is 800 miles away. The most distant is in Budapest."

"Budapest, Hungary? My daughter lived there for fourteen years."

"She married a television producer there. That's her permanent home now."

Joseph P. Smith

"You're a little short on close confidants, then. Do you belong to any clubs or such?"

"No. We used to belong to the country club when we both played golf. But it's been so long now, I wouldn't know anyone there."

"Is there a church?"

"Hungh! I haven't been to church since I got married."

"So there was a church somewhere in your past."

"Yes. My mother took me to church as a little child. I used to look forward to it. But as I grew up, I sort of drifted. We went to my childhood church to get married. It made my mother so proud. But we met in college, and his profession took us here. So I never got reconnected."

"You're life alone in that big house must be lonely."

"Yes. I don't even know who our neighbors are. My husband has lots of people he works with, but they never come to the house, and I rarely go to the office."

"Well. Let's turn from social resources to spiritual resources. Is God someone you can talk to?"

"You mean prayer. I do pray occasionally. It's usually in special problem times, when I'm afraid and don't know what to do."

"No regular prayer, at meals of bed-time?"

"Not in a long time."

"Tell me, when you think about God, what sort of image do you get? What is He like, to you?"

TALES FROM THE TOE TAG CHAPLAIN

"That's what's so hard about talking to him, for me. I really don't have any concept of what He is like. It's all so vague."

"Yes. That's a problem for all of us who aren't into idolatry. He knows what his God is like. We describe him in terms of what he isn't. He isn't visible; He doesn't have a body, etc. Or we describe him in terms so vast, that we can't comprehend them. Omnipotent, Omnipresent, or Omniscient. Those words just don't give you a picture, do they?"

"No, they don't."

"Well, that's why God gave us another way to picture Him. The Apostle Paul said it about Jesus. 'He is the image of the invisible God.'

The word image, in the original Greek language of the Bible, is Icon. In Greek churches, they won't depict saints and such in sculpture, but there are pictures they use, called icons. You never see the saints, but you see their pictures. Well, actually, no one knows what they looked like, so they're not really their picture. But they're something to focus on when you think about things you can't see.

I really don't think most icons are a good idea. When the same apostle talked about mankind's fall, he said, 'They exchanged the glory of the incorruptible God for an image in the form of corruptible man and of birds and four-footed animals and crawling creatures.

Instead, when God wanted to give us an icon to remind us about him, he showed us a living being, a person who could show what God was really like. That person was Jesus Christ.

Joseph P. Smith

Every person who understands the criteria by which historians separate reality from myth, knows that there was a real Jesus Christ. And the records of His life were written so soon after his death, that all sorts of people of that time could have denied that He existed. He really came into world history, and He claimed to be God in human flesh. As the famous author C. S. Lewis said, 'He was either a liar, a lunatic, or he is Lord.'

You can choose to focus on Him when you pray. He wants to be near you. He wants to strengthen your spirit, give you a powerful life, not as a victim of circumstances, but a victor over every enemy, even the last enemy which is death."

She replied, "He seems so far away, and so busy with things that I can't imagine Him caring about me."

"There's a reason He is so far away, and it isn't distance. God is holy. And we are not. We are all the product of a fallen human nature that wallows in selfishness. No one is as bad as we can imagine someone being, but there's no one who has never sinned in thought word or deed, and that separates us from God. He can't tolerate the stuff we do that makes His beautiful creation such a sea of suffering. If He didn't punish bad behavior, He wouldn't be holy, or righteous.

But to show us how terrible our sin is, and how He could accept us when we can't help ourselves, He sent Jesus to suffer the punishment for our sins, so he could accept us without becoming corrupted."

"I remember my Sunday School teacher talking about this."

Tales from The Toe Tag Chaplain

"Yes. What I've just told you is what Christians call the Gospel, the Good News. It's how we, just by trusting Him, can have a personal relationship with Him that begins now, and goes on for eternity!"

"But it's been so long.... It seems like a fairy tale."

"But it's not a myth. Jesus came in human flesh, lived the only perfect life, and died, not to pay for His own sin, but for yours and mine. He just asks you to trust Him."

"Thank you, Chaplain Smith, for this inspiring talk. I hope we meet again. But I need to rest now."

I hope to meet her in heaven. What she did with that witness is between her and God, right now. But to get to that witness, we had to go through a houseful of antiques.

Jesus wept. So the Jews were saying, "See how He loved him!" John 11:34-36

Chapter 27
The Sobbing Doctor

I was chiding my self for waiting for the elevator. My life was so involved in ministry that I wasn't getting enough exercise. And one of my self-inflicted remedies was to run the stairs, rather than riding the elevator. But I'd been up half the night in the ER, and I was tired.

Waiting for the car, I was thinking how strange it was that one of the remedies for lack of exercise was being skipped because I was tired. But there are different kinds of tired. My problem was not only a lack of exercise, but a lack of sleep.

Ding. The car arrived, the doors slid open, and self-absorbed, I got on without being aware of my surroundings.

When I finally looked up, I realized one of my favorite doctors was standing in the corner. My instinct was to greet him, but before I could, he turned his back to me and faced the corner. It seemed bizarre. He resembled a little boy being punished by standing in the corner.

Tales from The Toe Tag Chaplain

My words stuck in my throat as I tried to make sense of what I was seeing. My next reaction was to think this must be an ultimate snub. I'd gone straight to my rounds from the night in ER and hadn't showered. But I didn't think it was body odor. *What was going on!*

Then I saw it. His shoulders were rhythmically pulsing. He was sobbing! Realizing he didn't want to show it, I kept my silence and got off quickly at the cafeteria's floor, without looking back, feeling I had intruded on a very private moment.

But I couldn't get it off my mind. He must have headed for the men's room, because I didn't see him in the dining room.

I had come to the place in this ministry where tears were a daily occurrence. I wasn't ashamed of my tears, believing that my responsibility was to "weep with those who weep."

But Doctors aren't supposed to get emotional. It's important for them to maintain rationality, even when surrounded by tragedy.

I thought about the final illness of my wonderful mother-in-law. Her body was wracked with arthritis, and puffy with edema, water collected under her skin. She was in a little country hospital, twenty-five miles from my home. She couldn't turn herself in bed, and being turned frequently lowered the risk of pneumonia. But she was heavy, and her puffiness made it difficult to get hold of her. She couldn't help crying out in pain when anyone tried to move her.

I had often found the nurses in tears, unable to bring themselves to helpfully hurt her.

I was making the round trip to the hospital three times a day, just to turn her on the other side. Trying to be kind often turned out to be just the opposite. I had to learn to do the work quickly; get it over with, and ignore her cries. It wasn't easy.

Doctors often had to push themselves to do things that were oxymoronic, cruel kindness. Sentiment didn't serve them well.

But I remembered the emotional attachment of our country doctor that had saved my second daughter's life. And it gave me a idea of how to help my doctor friend.

That evening I went home and hand wrote a letter of several pages to the doctor. It went something like this.

I saw you struggling with grief in the elevator today, and I didn't want to intrude on your private moment. But even though it usually serves a doctor well to be stoic all the time, there was one time when a doctor's emotional struggle helped save the life of our second daughter.

Just twenty-eight days after she was born, my little (4'-11 ¾ ") wife was holding her in her arms near my desk in the room of the rambling farm-house parsonage I used for my study, when suddenly the baby vomited on the ten foot high ceiling. Although I had never seen projectile vomiting before, I had been told about it, because I had two brothers with pyloric stenosis, and had been told about the symptoms.

Being sure of what the problem was, I called the hospital to tell them we were coming, got a baby sitter for child number one, and my wife and I drove her to the country hospital that was twenty-five miles away. It was Sunday evening, but our wonderful doctor met us at the door, listened to our story, explained that no doubt it was pyloric stenosis, and said they'd make her comfortable for the night. Then a radiologist who came once a week, on Monday, from the state hospital, would confirm the diagnosis, they'd operate, and she'd be fine.

We stayed the night and were with her when they took her for an upper GI the next morning. Our doctor came in shortly after the baby came back, and told us that the x-ray showed the barium passing the pyloric valve, and that meant it wasn't what we thought.

Joseph P. Smith

The baby couldn't keep anything down and was dehydrating. There were no veins formed yet where they could give her fluids intravenously, so they stuck a large needle in her upper leg muscles to try to hydrate her that way. It wasn't working.

Our doctor couldn't ethically operate for something where the x-rays were negative, and as days went on and the baby got weaker, he got more worried.

Finally, on Thursday he came in and said he hadn't slept all night, and in desperation told us to take our baby out of this hospital, take her someplace else, and not to tell anybody about the x-ray.

The baby was so weak she couldn't clear her throat and was in danger of choking. We had to take a nurse with us to aspirate her throat. But we went an additional thirty-five miles to a university hospital.

They had a new invention, a positive pressure pump that could put fluids in an artery, and immediately started infusions in an artery in her scalp. That done, they ordered an upper GI, confirmed the diagnosis, operated and she was well enough to go home in two days.

That girl is a high-school volleyball player today, and has a burning desire to be a teacher, all because a doctor got emotional.

Tales from The Toe Tag Chaplain

I sealed the letter in an envelope, put it inside the pages of Philip Yancey's book, "Where is God When It Hurts" and put it in the Doctor's internal mail box.

He never acknowledged it to me, but I found out that he belonged to a book club where all the members read the same book once a month, and met to talk about it. He recommended Yancey's book.

That was thanks enough, and it still allowed his privacy.

He who descended is Himself
also He who ascended
far above all the heavens,
so that He might fill all things.)
Ephesians 4:10

Chapter 28
Caroling, Caroling

Holidays, like milestones, mark our travel through life. Just a month from today as I write this, I will be 81 years old. And for the first time in 21 years, I will be near enough to half of my children so it won't be lonely.

The marking of time by holidays is important for those who have only a short time to live. Year after year, twice as many people died in our department in January as died in December. Life is prolonged by looking forward to something.

Of all the losses in the dreary experience of slowly dying, the one that is most poignant is the loss of hope. Even Christians, who have the blessed hope of seeing Jesus face-to-face, often struggle with having to adjust their hopes to look forward to things that are not of this world.

Tales from The Toe Tag Chaplain

> Now faith is the assurance
> of *things* hoped for,
> the conviction of things not seen.
> Hebrews 11:1

Knowing this, the staff of our department went to great lengths to celebrate Christmas. Our floor was laid out as a cross, and at the end of each corridor they put a medium sized Christmas tree. The lights and tinsel glittered down all the areas outside of the rooms. A larger tree was positioned in the family visiting area, near the center of the cross, and diagonally across from the charting area.

Since many patients never saw the hallways, they decided to wrap the doors with Christmas paper and wide ribbons, each festooned with giant bows. As patients began to react positively to this, other steps were taken. Eggnog as well as cider was kept in the department refrigerator, and offered to patients at snack time.

All this was done without any funds from the hospital. In the holiday spirit, we dug deep to maximize holiday cheer.

Then they had the crowning idea. *Why don't we have a Christmas Carol sing? We can*

Joseph P. Smith

bring all the patients who want to come down to the family area. Family members could be invited to join us.

We looked for a staff member with a guitar, and found an old navy nurse, whose mouth was so "salty" that she couldn't say pass the butter without describing its sex life. But she was sure she could play the cords.

Parameters were set. It would only be 20 minutes long. Patients would have to sign a release if they wanted to come. The logistics of transport were worked out.

Some patients could walk. Some could be wheeled down. These were counted and it was arranged where we could borrow wheelchairs. One could only be moved in a gurney, and had to be lifted to it from the bed with a Hoyer Lift. That would follow her down the hall so she could be moved to a recliner in the family area.

Chairs would be slid down the corridors so all patients could sit. Family members would stand behind their loved ones.

Invitations to family members were made in the copier and distributed a week in advance. Everybody had an assignment. Staff from other shifts would come in on their own time to help. Our goal was to move everybody in five minutes, sing carols for 20 minutes, and have everything back to normal in just a total of one-half hour. We were sure we could do it from 2:00 to 2:30 on the 22nd of December.

Then, on that very morning, someone decided to ask administration's permission. The request, complete with the logistical plan, ended up on the desk of a corporate lawyer. He wasn't worried about safety, but concerned that we might offend some non-Christians. He refused permission.

The only adjective I could think of to describe the department was "thunderstruck."

"How will we tell the other shifts not to come in? What about family members, some coming as much as 150 miles? " And most of all, "What will this do to our patients, who are all looking forward to it.?"

A dozen of the staff gathered near the Unit desk, questioning how to proceed. "Let's go on strike," was the first suggestion.

But then a wiser head said, "No. We should have worked this out in advance and negotiated permission. But the administration has their backsides covered with this letter. They're not going to physically stop us. So let's just do it!"

As the clock struck two, the team swung into action. At 2:05 everyone was in place, but the patient who came on a gurney was still being lowered into the recliner. About 25 family members stood behind their loved ones, many with hands on their shoulders. Where there was room at the end of the row, a father squatted by the wheelchair of his son.

Three nurses knelt on the floor by the tree, one with the guitar, another with the trained soprano voice that sang arias from "Messiah" at her college's Christmas program. The third held poster board signs with the lyrics, and made up for her lack of talent with her passion. Tears were pouring down her cheeks as we sang, *Silent Night, Hark the Herald Angels, Away in a Manger*" and finally, *What Child is This?*

Some struggled to sing with lungs filled with tumors. Others beamed at the crowd. All of us felt a common bond of celebration together.

The 20 minutes passed quickly and with the same almost military precision everyone was whisked back to their rooms and all evidence of this unauthorized event was gone.

Except for one thing! There was a joy in our department that belied the grim reality that

for 23 of our patients this was their last
Christmas on earth!

Joseph P. Smith

Afterward

Of course, there are too many stories that I could have told. These are only some that I prominently remember from nearly 30 years ago.

I suppose this is the place where I'm supposed to show the theme that holds them all together. But the truth is, there is no such theme.

If there is one thing I can say that makes these stories hang together, it is that they represent reality, and that has infinite variety.

Perhaps this is not the most important ministry in the world. It certainly is a short-term ministry. You are left to wonder about its long-term effect. But the short term needs you meet are very significant steps on the way to heaven. I am glad my wonderful Lord allowed me to share them with magnificent people.

TALES FROM THE TOE TAG CHAPLAIN

Joe Smith is available to speak in your church or other gathering. To book an appearance, call 616-531-1840 or go to hospitalchaplain@ifca.org.

If this book piques your interest in hospital chaplaincy, contact the author for help and advice.

Made in the USA
Charleston, SC
17 November 2013